GOD

POSSIBILITIES

Forty-Eight Questions
to the
Guidance of God

Tom Golinski

Please recognize that I am on my path.

And it is not necessary that it look

the same as yours.

The capitalization of certain words simply

felt right in the moments they

were received.

I am beginning to learn to lighten up.

To the family I would come to know.

CONTENTS

Introduction....................(From Guidance)

Part I

Questions:

Contents (cont.)

Part II

Questions:

Contents (cont.)

Introduction
(From Guidance)

Outside of God is only chaos. And outside of chaos has God organized Himself as All Love relating to all love. Thus has God extracted all meaning from all potential chaos, establishing anything that does not appear to be within Himself as meaningless. What cannot be used within the living process of All Love relating to all love is released to the nothingness that remains as potential without meaningful purpose. Therefore it has no potential at all.

PART I

Jesus Who Is The Christe

Am I forgiven?

Not yet. For you have not yet forgiven me. All forgiveness resides within your mind, which is the only place forgiveness, or any other thought, can be for you. I reside there with you, as does everyone else and all of creation. You have not forgiven me because you cannot conceive of the idea that you continually participate in all of creation, and therefore refuse to take responsibility for what you believe you see and experience now. Thus you project blame to others, to me, and to God.

You do not realize the extent to which you participate in the making of the world you see. Yet, by definition, the world *you see* would not exist at all without your participation. Thus it must be clear that the world you think you see is merely an opinion and projection of what you believe is outside of you. Yet if everything is experienced in the mind, and it indeed is, then anything you envision cannot really be outside of you, since your own mind has envisioned it.

You are beginning to grasp the idea now that all thoughts that *you* have must be in *your* mind, including your own opinions about what you think you see and experience. However you are unable to fathom the idea that you have somehow helped *bring forth* what you seem to see and experience in the world. But remember, *the* world *is* your world as you see it. That is all you have made; simply an opinion of what you think you see and experience. This opinion is relative only to you, as is the world you think you see. This world you made has absolutely no reality to anyone else, unless it happens to coincide with opinions others may have about "realities" also in their own worlds. Here dreams seem to coincide, but they still do not create reality.

This is the separated state from which you ask the question, "Am I forgiven?" Yet you expect an answer that is meaningful to you and wonder why you do not seem to receive it. Can you see that any answer you receive within your world of opinion would only be an additional opinion? Yet even this you require, for this is the only world you see, and thus the only place you think you can be forgiven.

And in this you are correct. You appear to be in your own little dream world of your own making. And it is from this you must escape. You believe it is your reality, for it appears as such to you. It seems inconceivable to you that you have made your life, and your world, what you have wanted them to be, and given them all the meaning they seem to have. But you have done so. And now you wish for something more, because you realize it is not enough.

It is from this dream world of perceptions, opinions, and judgments, from which you ask forgiveness. There is a world of reality beyond the one you have constructed, but you cannot see it, because you stand condemned within the world you seem to have made and believe is real.

So now we must ask some questions. What do you want? Can you answer honestly? You say you want something more than what you have. But do you just want a better dream world? Do you want to add to the "reality" of the life that you have made in a world of your own creation? Do you ask forgiveness because you have reached a barricade in your world and want it cleared, so you can move on "creating" as you have done in the past?

Who can give you a better dream but you, since it is you who is dreaming? Would you want to fix the dream you made by asking someone *else* to fix it? How would they know it would be to your liking within your dream? And would you ask them for forgiveness? What would they forgive you *for*?

These are many questions that distill into one. Do you wish to remain in the world you think you see? You cannot escape a dream of condemnation that you have made, unless you receive your own forgiveness. God does not condemn an act of dreaming, nor do I. The word condemnation has meaning only within your dream. A child is not condemned for having a nightmare.

But now you protest, for you have harmed others in your dream. And surely you cannot accept that you made them up and they have no existence on their own. Nothing has existence "on its own." Yet you have never witnessed other's realities. You have only seen bits and pieces of their dreams, which coincided and intermingled with your own. This does not make them real.

And within your mind is where it all takes place. So it must be from within your mind that forgiveness comes. You can receive it nowhere else, for it is the place from which you have condemned yourself. It is the place from which you have condemned all others, along with your image of what you think God is, and what you think I am.

You still seek my forgiveness? You have it. God's forgiveness was never possible, for His condemnation never existed except within your dreaming. My condemnation of you was only in your dreaming as well, so now you are set free of it. Yet I ask forgiveness of your dreaming mind on behalf of myself, God, and all "others" you may perceive. For you cannot escape your own dream unless you are free to leave it from within. And you will never leave it while you are so heavily attached by your own condemnation.

Jesus Who is the Christ

What is the truth?

You do well to ask this question, because it expresses your understanding that you do not know what truth is, as well as expressing your desire to know. You would also do well to remember this as I respond, or you will not be open to receive an answer outside of your current belief system.

There is a question behind your question. You really want to know if the guidance you hear from *me* is truth. This raises the question of not only what I am, but also what you are in relation to me. You want to know if I am the truth and, if so, why would I share it with you who believe that you are not, and why have I not shared it with you before.

Dimly, you are beginning to realize that you did not want to hear it before. You were very busy making your own world in your own mind, discovering your own truths and incorporating them into your expanding personal belief system. These became part of your personality, and ultimately helped establish what you think you are. It is from this place that you ask the question, "What is the truth?" Part of you wants to receive some tremendous all encompassing revelation of truth. But beneath this is the assumption that it will somehow fit neatly into your current belief system so you can comprehend it.

Yet if truth is universal there must be some way to comprehend it, even within a very personal and very limited belief system. And there is. Truth is simple. It is love expressed. Yet words are merely symbols. They do not mean anything unless they inspire the reality behind them. Explaining truth to someone is meaningless unless at some point they have *felt* the reality of truth. Love, as a word, is meaningless unless you *feel* the reality of love. When you do, there is no question of its reality or truthfulness in the moment. And in the moment is the only "time" that truth, love, and reality can be experienced, as well as anything else. Truth is love expressed in the moment.

Let us apply this to your question behind your question. Is the guidance you receive from me the truth? You will feel it. Or not. When you feel the guidance as loving, with *no other* motivation but your best interest at heart, no matter how the words or ideas may or may not fit into your current limited belief system, then they are truthful and of me. If not, they have been skewed, changed, or replaced by your own personal limited mindset. You will refuse to believe what you refuse to make room for within your belief system. You must literally be willing to make room for what currently appears to be beyond your belief. Do you see that otherwise you will never change? You will refuse to abandon your established "truths."

So now I hear your question. If truth is love expressed in the moment, then is my life relegated to bits and scraps of both truth and love, for neither seem to endure in my world? And of course you have answered your own question. You have made a personal world that seems to be absent of both truth and love, except for fleeting moments. Yet it is your world. And you prize it dearly because you have made it. You have borne witness to its reality through all the "senses" of the body, which you have called your own identity. And you witness other bodies that bear witness to your own, some of which seem more sinful and some less.

You still cannot comprehend that you see the world that you want to see and that you experience the truths that you want to be true. In this, you have no idea of the power of your own mind. Yet it is this same power that will lead you to truth. Can you see that this *must* happen when you simply change what you *want*? Do you *want* to see everyone in your world as totally innocent, without the slightest trace of guilt to tarnish what you would behold? You say this is impossible in this world of chaos and havoc. You do not realize that this simply attests to the fact that you are not yet ready to suspend your belief system to make room for another, which is benign and sweet and inclusive and sharing and simply awaits your desire to see it. Not in addition to the world you now think you see, but to replace it.

How many worlds do you think there can be in creation? Would you dare put a number to it? Are they unreal, while the one you see remains the only real one? Where do they *all* exist? Where are they *all* experienced? In mind, and nowhere else. For what is not experienced does not exist at all. And all experience is experienced in the mind of the one who would perceive. You make up the world you think you "see" outside of you and make a body with senses to perceive the thoughts you have projected out. Where can your body be *experienced* but in your mind, the clearing ground for all experience. Yet as long as you believe that changing your mind will not change your reality, these are all wasted words.

Can you see that if you knew you were absolutely innocent and totally guilt free, you would have no thought whatsoever of projecting guilt into a world of your own making, just so you could feel relatively better about yourself? You could project only a loving world, for love is what you would be.

And that is what you *are*. That is your reality, no matter how many worlds you wish to project in your games of guilt. Surely you now see that none of them are real. None of them exist beyond your own mind's attachment to them. And you would not attach to them if you did not believe you are guilty. You have projected what is in your mind, and it looks like a guilty world.

Thus we have made a full circle back to your earlier question, "Am I Forgiven?" So I must reassure you once more that you indeed are forgiven, for you have never sinned, except in your own dream world. And those you think accuse you there are in *your* mind. Forgive them and forgive yourself and forgive your world. It has served you simply as it has served you, and now you can move on.

What is truth? *You* are truth. This you will know when you escape your personal dream world with guilt as its foundation, and guilt as its projection. Truth is love expressed. You are love expressed, except in your dreams of guilt and sin. I am the truth of your mind returned to love. Your whole Mind is there and never left. It resides there with all of creation. This Mind is shared by all of creation. All of creation interacts with itself only through love, which is truth expressed. They are the same.

When it is this you want more than your private personal world of your mind's own making, you will find it beyond the little stretch of time you think you carved out of eternity for yourself alone. The truth of you waits in eternity for the child who dreamed he fell in the mud on the way home.

Jesus Who Is The Christ

What does it mean to "Become as a little child?"

It means that you acknowledge you do not understand reality and that *you are willing to learn.*

By becoming a little child in your heart, you are able to recognize, and access, a clean new birthing place from which you will be able to perceive a clean, new, and innocent world of reality. A world totally free of the useless clutter, conflict, and confusion that you placed there through years of adherence and addiction to an ego driven thought system based upon fear, survival, and separation. Even within these few words I give you, you are able to begin to comprehend the vast potential, power, and significance for you, if you are willing to become as a little child.

Your thought now simply is, "But this would be make believe." Yet in your heart you do not believe this. You are becoming more and more aware that the world you have believed in, and established as your version of your life, is the one that has been make believe all along. You are beginning to realize and accept that the only reality you have *ever* experienced in your self made world was every loving thought you ever felt, experienced, and shared. In fact, each loving thought is always shared because it radiates its own clarity and purity, from heart and mind to all creation. And all creation is of love and must receive its own communication.

There are no limits to what a little child can be and do and experience, especially when you realize the little child is your mind, released of all judgment, and therefore all condemnation. It is pure acceptance and it is pure trust.

And here is where you believe you have a problem. It lies within this word, this concept called trust. For it implies faith. And the two cannot be apart in your mind. In your perception, you believe you have exhibited very little trust, because you have felt very little faith, if any. Your mind reels at the monumental undertaking it would surely be for you to somehow produce, out of nowhere, this faith and trust. You feel you have shown no past ability to establish such characteristics, much less hold them. With this lack of evidence, the "task" seems hopeless.

Yet listen closely to me now. In your life as *you* have experienced it, you have demonstrated tremendous faith, building gradually from the time that you actually knew yourself as a little child. You developed faith in the experiences you believe you received, but much more so from your *interpretation* of what those experiences meant to you. You had to *decide* what those experiences meant. Then you judged them to be good or bad or right or wrong to *you.* You birthed judgment relative to yourself alone, because all the teaching and learning you received was that you *were* alone. You were a separate being destined to make your way through an ever expanding and often ever more dangerous world. You may have been told that you could achieve anything "in the world," but you developed much more faith in the concept that you *were* alone. This faith was restored and reinforced every time a loved one died or a dream was shattered. And finally, your identification of yourself as a body gave you faith in death and time.

You have lived your life with faith always as your guide. There is no question of this. The real question for you is only, "What have I been faithful to?" You know the answer. You have been faithful to the self you made in your own mind. You had so much faith in it, that you believed it was you. Think how much faith was required that you could build a world around a self you made, and then call it reality.

Yet there were problems with the self you made, even though you attached it to a body and used all the body's senses to confirm to you that the self and the world you made were true. You did not trust them. If they were reality, they were at best capricious and uncaring, and at worst would overtly attack and destroy you. You found you had to defend yourself against what you had put all your faith in. You finally are beginning to realize you have no trust in what you have been faithful to. So it must not be true. And so it must be a lie.

You have not wasted a life. Neither yours nor anyone else's. You have simply been misguided. You used a make believe self as a guide. There is no blame and there is no loss. For loss and blame can only appear to be experienced within time. And time does not fit into your reality.

How can you become as a little child? Withdraw faith in your self-made "reality." You do not trust it, and you know it is not real. When you withdraw faith in it totally, you will have removed every trace of guilt you have ever felt and endlessly relived. The need for it is gone because the reality of it has disappeared. Then you will know your innocence and know that innocence has always been your reality. The nightmare will be over.

And the child will be reborn.

Jesus Who Is The Christ

Have I paid my dues?

You have many questions behind this question, but they all merge into one, "Have I suffered enough in hell?"

You received a recent vision, in a dream, indicating that you had indeed paid your dues, and it was now time to enjoy your life. You heard, "Now we've been way too serious. We've got to have more fun." This messenger was announced to you as if through a television screen directed at you only. He was represented as, "the vice president," even while appearing to be wearing a turban. This dream had great impact upon you, and you took this messenger to be a very powerful, though somewhat lighthearted, representation of a second in command.

Deeper within your question lies a powerful vision you experienced earlier in your life, before you embarked upon you current spiritual path. This vision was clearly of a man who represented Jesus very deliberately walking up a grassy hillside, in a state of serious and deep contemplation, as if bearing the weight of the world. You were simply a bystander in this vision until he stopped, turned his head, and directed a portion of his attention toward you. You felt the overwhelming power of this being. And within that instant you perceived that Jesus was deciding whether your existence should or should not continue. You received the clear message, "DO SOMETHING!" The figure of Jesus then returned his attention to where it had been and continued forward, up the hillside.

You have felt many interpretations of this message but generally you deemed it to be that somehow, somewhere in your life, there was a purpose not being fulfilled, and without its fulfillment your life must be relatively meaningless. Perhaps there was a grand plan if you could find it. This vision did not particularly encourage you to seek God. The figure within it was powerful but fearful. You had no desire to emulate this version of Jesus. But you had received a message. And to you, a key element of this message was that in some way you must apparently pay your dues. You must justify the life you are living in the world you see, and complete your purpose satisfactorily, before you can move on. And if you are stuck and cannot move on, that would be hell.

Now we arrive at the real meaning of your question. "Have I been crucified enough, or is there more to come?" The man, Jesus, was crucified in a time of what you call the past. You were very careful when you called upon me to address me as Jesus Who is the Christ. It had to be very clear to you that I represented the risen Christ, and not your earlier vision of a Jesus who did not seem free, and who could condemn.

You have long neither considered yourself a good Christian nor religious. Yet you have also long considered yourself condemned. You would not believe in a God who could condemn. But you held tightly to your belief in a self that could. And so you pay the consequences of this belief. You condemn and believe you are condemned in return, and you are haunted by your own condemnation. These thoughts are the dues you think you have been paying. And these thoughts are the dues you believe you may still have to pay.

Now you want to know if Jesus, or Christ, or God wants you to have these thoughts and maintain them. This is what you really ask when you ask if you have paid your dues. God is real, but love does not condemn. Christ is real and is the Son of God. You may find other terminology resonates within you. Words never matter as long as the meaning is not obscured. You are real as well. But your reality is only what is of God and Christ. All the rest you have made up. Your mind has tremendous power. But it cannot make of God and Christ what They are not.

Nor can it make of you what you are not. You are free to play in dreams and in nightmares of condemnation. They will seem real enough to you. But you cannot create a vengeful god and make it real. When your fear of a vengeful god is gone, you will be free to know God and we will be one in Christ. You will remember you have always been the Son of God, from which nothing has been excluded. And you will know that this is your due.

Jesus Who Is The Christ

When I awaken in mind, what will be of my
family and friends?

You cannot awaken to *less* than what you had
when you were asleep. You can only awaken to the
reality of those you thought you knew in your
dreams. You only experienced fragments of their
true realities. Those fragments of their realities are
represented by every loving thought you ever had
about them or they about you, all of which are
shared, whether you believe you were aware of it at
the time or not.

You believe that somehow you are being a
traitor to your family and friends because you seem
to be seeking more than they are able to provide.
This seems to display your lack of gratitude for what
you already have. But beneath this is your feeling
that *you* have not provided enough for *them*. And
now you have discovered another source for your
generous reservoir of guilt.

You want to take them with you in your mind
as you awaken, but you do not realize that it is
within your mind that you have imprisoned them.
You do not really know them. You have built images
of who you think they are in your mind and it is
these images that you believe is their reality. Yet
you are beginning to understand that you do not
recognize your *own* reality. The nature of true

communication is unconditional love. When it is this you are experiencing with friends and family, you are sharing a glimpse of reality.

You find it difficult to conceive of communication that flows *only* from unconditional love to unconditional love, but no other kind of communication exists in reality. Thus no other kind of communication really exists at all. All other attempts are simply efforts made to communicate by those who speak different languages. Without the commonality of love, true communication is an illusion.

Would you know the reality of family and friends in this world? Set them free. Then the world will change. Your world will change, and their worlds will change. Then you will be free to share love, where minds and hearts are joined. And this *is* a new world of freedom. Everyone will be free to be free. No one will be imprisoned by anothers thoughts of what they should be, how they should act, or who or what they are. Perhaps you would also choose to set free the friends and loved ones who appear to have exited your world before you.

Is it this kind of freedom you would give your family and friends? For this is the freedom of each one's reality, as well as yours. When free beings join in this reality, they become as one. And love is experienced and expanded exponentially. This is Heaven. And each meeting and joining is a heavenly event. And your world is healed.

Jesus Who Is The Christ

What is my question now?

You have one question that you must ask before you can proceed, but you fear that by asking it, you will offend me. Your question is, "Are you the one to whom I should be addressing these questions?"

You have been asking questions of the Holy Spirit in recent years and have received what you perceive to be mixed results. Rather unexpectedly, you found yourself asking the question, "Am I forgiven?" of the entity you called, Jesus Who is the Christ. And I responded to you. Now I refer you to the answer I gave to your question, "What is the truth?" before responding to the one you are now concerned with.

But your question requires additional response. You want to know from whom you should receive your guidance, because you are somewhat confused. You wish to receive the truth. This is a genuine request within your current understanding. However, your present ability to comprehend truth still lies within the parameters of your willingness to receive it. This depends on the rigidity of your current belief system. Once again, you will not believe what you refuse to believe.

What if I told you that the differences you perceive between the Holy Spirit and myself are differences you established in your own mind? You determine what guides you are most open to hearing within your own belief system. The names you use are only as valuable to you as the meanings you perceive within them.

You feel you were led away from the man, Jesus, as your guide, not only from childhood images of him crucified on a cross, but also from your vivid dream of him as a fearsome, and thus fearful, being. Your other limited religious exposures did not resonate with you, but you began to realize there had to be more to life than the pains and pleasures of a gradual, but certain, road to death. It was a "New Age" and many spiritual paths seemed to become available. Eventually you settled upon one in which the Holy Spirit played a prominent role. You could accept this. It was much less threatening to you, even if somewhat less personal.

In your mind, and not without valid reasons, you perceive the Holy Spirit to represent every answer to every question within eternity. That is, the Holy Spirit represents the connecting link between God as All That Is, and everything that seems to not be *aware* it is part of All That Is. You tend to perceive Christ as representing the reality of all of humanity and all that humanity interacts with. Thus the Holy Spirit seems more all encompassing to you and the Christ, as the Son of God representing all of humanity, seems more personal.

Having the Holy Spirit as your guide was not only acceptable to you until now, but also preferable, since you were not willing to commit totally to the spiritual path. A seemingly less personal relationship subconsciously represented a buffer against being suddenly swept away into ascension and rudely and abruptly pulled from your personal world. You wanted something more, but not all at once.

Asking a serious and honest question of Jesus as the Christ is a significant change for you, marking the reduction of the defenses you had established to keep God at a "safe" distance. Not only is Christ more personal than the Holy Spirit for you, but also invoking the name of Jesus in your question signifies your willingness to accept within your belief system that the essence of humanity can attain divinity. Not withstanding the fact that this essence already *is* divinity.

It is important for you to understand that God has not been hiding from you. Christ is not hiding from you, and the Holy Spirit will be as personal as you will allow. You are the one who has been playing hide and seek, but you have been lost only in your own mind. You think you cannot find your way out. But call in *complete* sincerity and your own Identity will gently guide you to freedom. And the form it takes will be the one that you can hear.

Jesus Who Is The Christ

What is my question now?

What you are expressing is that my answer to your previous question was not adequate, in the sense that it did not give you full peace of mind. Specifically, you perceive my noting of your willingness to somewhat lower your defenses against God as also a willingness to *align* yourself with a man called Jesus, and that he represented, or represents, the process of the essence of humanity attaining divinity. In other words, your concern is basically that you must do what Jesus has done in order to ascend. This raises the identical question that was really asked in your query about paying dues, "Have I been crucified enough, or is there more to come?"

At this point, it is important to point out that your understanding of Jesus is what you have established within your own personal belief system. We have stated that it is only the meaning behind words that has value. The meaning you have assigned to the name of Jesus is much more associated with a fearful image of sacrifice, crucifixion, and death than one of love, resurrection, and life. Some of the reasons for this we have already shared. Thus becoming closer to your past concept or idea of Jesus is still more fearful than peaceful.

Fear tends to freeze you in time. As long as you are fearful, you cannot proceed in a meaningful way, except perhaps into more fear, which will indeed seem meaningful to you. Fear has no meaning in reality, but within your dream it appears to be the controlling factor.

I have already told you that love cannot condemn, but the idea of sacrifice is still very real to you. As long as you believe your reality is a body within the world you see, the idea of sacrifice will remain with you. You do not realize how steadfastly you cling to it. This is because you cannot comprehend a self and a world created of, and by, only love. Nothing more, nothing less.

Your image of what you believe Jesus represents will change. Until it does, it will remain an obstacle to your escape from the world you made. My purpose is to help make your path clear, not to allow obstacles to become more solid in your mind because you are not yet ready to let them go.

So now I acknowledge your real desire. And that is to address me in a manner you feel more comfortable with. You wish to address me as, "Christ Who is complete." You view Christ as not only the reality of all of humanity, but also as the culmination of every prodigal son's journey home. In other words, this Christ is beyond time entirely. Because you now realize that all apparent physical journeys occur within a timeline, you know this must include yours. It is a story. It is the story of you and the world you see. You seek guidance from an entity outside of time that already experiences the reality of you as having arrived home. You seek guidance from that which knows your journey is already over, in reality.

What this accomplishes for you, to a degree, is the ability to believe that you actually *will* arrive "home." This assurance I can give you now, or God would not be All That Is. How could God be complete while missing even one aspect of Itself?

You are making significant progress on your dream journey through time, because you are willing to let go of more and more barriers you have constructed in "protection" of the world you made.

You have asked and you shall receive. Please feel free to address me as, "Christ Who is complete." You will meet your Self within me.

Christ Who Is Complete

Why does suffering and sacrifice still seem real?

You might as easily ask why the world you see still seems real, for they are the same question.

As long as you see yourself as a separate self within a self envisioned world, the ideas of suffering and sacrifice will still have meaning for you and will still be experienced as part of your personal reality. You think that I or the Holy Spirit or God should be able to rid them from your reality for you. Yet you are still not willing to relinquish your version of reality. Thus you would want God to enter your dream and clean up what you do not like within it.

This you have heard described as attempting to bring light to the darkness. Light does dispel darkness, but Light also respects all things, including the dream self you have made and the world it seems to play within. Would you have the Light of God dispel the darkness you perceive in your dream and yet leave you there within it? You can surely see that this would only serve to reinforce the reality of your dream. God does not recognize your dream because God did not create it. God creates only love joined with love. Nothing else exists in reality. As we have said, the only reality of your dream lies in moments of love expressed. All the rest is your own game of separation.

Would you have a powerful guide perform the function God will not provide for you within the dream? This would appear as magic. Your mind, even in its limited awareness, is powerful enough to do magic. After all, it has made the world you think you see appear to be the *only* world that exists, and leads you to believe that you can actually comprehend it with some sort of accuracy. All this from the viewpoint of a tiny spec of a self among billions of separate other selves. Perhaps a powerful guide could somehow sort this all out for you.

A loving Guide does not originate from within the dream itself, but comes with the sole purpose of leading you out of the dream entirely. For this, no magic is required, but miracles of joining will abound. Yet this Guide is available in response only to your invitation. If It forced itself upon you, It would be a tyrant and not a guide at all. You will not be pulled from your carefully constructed dream in terror and fear of loss without your consent.

And this indeed addresses the essence of your question. You fear the "dark night of the soul." Yet if it were one night, you would accept it gladly. In times of agony, even death you do not fear, and would accept it gladly as well. But you have been told, and are now beginning to comprehend, that death is not real. It is not death, but a life of suffering and sacrifice you fear. The "death by a thousand cuts" would not even lead to its promised reward. This fear of suffering and sacrifice is not just for your physical self, but also for anyone and anything you *value* in the world you perceive as real.

You fear the loss of what you value in your world, but there is a thought beneath this wherein the potential terror lies. You fear the Last Judgment. You fear God. You remind yourself that God is love, but just as quickly remind yourself that you are not. Not yet. Not *only* love and nothing else.

So how will your world be dismantled? How much pain and agony will there be? And above all, how long will it take? How many lifetimes before you are good enough and holy enough to escape time itself? Is there one final test? So perhaps it is just as well that you remain in the dream.

But you cannot. It is not enough anymore. You know that you would be living an illusion that is a lie. And you are tired of it. You believe that you are trapped; trapped in your own mind with no way to get out on your own. And you are correct. So best of luck to you.

But wait! Be of good cheer! I am here. You have *never* been alone. But you did an excellent job of pretending that you were. I will not butt in on your pretending. But know that I am here and always have been.

You will not be ripped by the roots out of your dream. That is, not unless you do it to yourself. And you could. You are free to do so. And then you would experience terror. You are also in charge of how much time it will take, and by what means it will be that your dream is dismantled. You will choose to do it yourself, as you constructed it, or you will ask for help. I suggest you ask for help.

You have been playing a game of hide and seek, thinking you built a private world and a separate self. And what you think you are got lost in what you made. When you become as a little child, you will accept that you do not know where you are or what you are doing. The woods may still seem dark and dangerous but you know there is One Who will show you the way out. There is a test that you can administer to yourself at any time. You can ask, "How much do I value the world I see, and how much do I believe in its reality?" Then you can ask, "How much do I want it to *stay* that way?" Your answers will provide a fear and terror index that you can monitor to determine how heavily your world weighs upon you.

Perhaps you should lighten up. It could be that you have been way too serious. It might be time to begin having more fun.

Christ Who Is Complete

Is the world an image only in my mind?

Although on the surface this idea seems utterly unbelievable and absurd to you, on a deeper level, you can already accept it. You can already acknowledge the idea that what appears real to you in the world you see is based on your interpretation of what reality is, and on your unwillingness to perceive a world without your preconceived and personal judgments attached. That is, the world you see has relevance only from the perspective of yourself within it. The world you see would not exist without you included. So where is the reality of the world?

Enter your mind. Please do. There is nowhere else to be. There is nowhere else for a world to be. Except there is to you. You have taken your image of a world and projected it "outward" from your mind's awareness as if onto a giant three dimensional theatre screen in the round, with the addition of up and down. You may say this is not a fair comparison, since your body's senses of touch and smell and taste will expose the unreality of what sight and sound reflect within this theatre. Yet you know within your heart that it is only a matter of time before technology in your world will perfect virtual three-dimensional experiences that seem totally real. Which realities will *be* real?

That the world you see is a projection is not beyond your current belief system. What you have difficulty accepting is that *you* could have projected it from a source beyond your present consciousness. Furthermore you believe you certainly could not have done this alone, since "others" seem to acknowledge the same world you see. If the world as you know it is an illusion, then there must have been some fantastic collaboration of gigantic proportion that has taken place, and is still taking place, which is entirely outside of your control. Therefore you cannot be held accountable for how it turned out. The world may be a mess, but you are not to blame for it. This mess of a world must be someone else's projection. You do not kill people and cause wars. You are just a bystander and witness to the carnage.

Now I will tell you that you are a participant, not a bystander. Where does this carnage take place? Seemingly in the world. Where does this world take place? In your mind. You could not *see* carnage in *any* world if you were not a participant within your own mind. You accept the ideas of suffering, sacrifice, and pain, and any other form carnage may seem to take for you, as *real*. But they are unbearable, so you project them out onto an imaginary world in order to get rid of them. But you are not rid of them. It is just that you wish to be innocent, so therefore others in the world must be guilty.

Then why do you still feel guilty? Because you are a participant. What is an act of war, except an extension of a *thought* of war? What is an act of killing, if not an extension of the *thought* to kill? Perhaps we should look at your thoughts. And perhaps you are beginning to see how you are a participant. If you are angry with others, what are your thoughts about them? Do you wish them eternal blissful life? What if you believe you have been a victim of a heinous act? Is punishment required, not in vengeance, but in the name of "justice?" What if you treat another unfairly? Where does your guilt go?

You know these thoughts are projected out of "you" and into your world. If you held on to them cumulatively without an outlet, you believe they would destroy you. You could not bear to retain the totality of them in your own mind. Surely the world can absorb them with relatively little harm. Yet where is your world? It is in your own mind. There is no other world to absorb them for you except the one you made. A circle is completed that has escaped your conscious thinking.

So what do you do? What are your choices? Will forgiveness take care of all this and bring you back to innocence? Yes it will, but not if you believe that all of the projections of your dream world actually happened in reality. For if death actually is real, how can you forgive the dead back to life? If everyone in your dream world is a child of God, then how can they suffer, when God is only love? Perhaps

God is not love or your world is not real. One of those two viewpoints is true. Which one do you *want* to be true?

If you think God is not love, then you will see a world that is not loving. And you will see this because it is what you want to see. If you want to see a different world not of your making, then you will need help, because you are so heavily invested in the one you made. If you feel as if no help is really available, then you have decided that love is not real and your world is. And it will be you and your world versus reality.

You may choose to establish and continue this conflict within your mind, but there is one thing of which you may be assured. We who await your call for guidance can find no possible cause for suspense as to the ultimate outcome. There is no conflict in reality.

Christ Who Is Complete

Have I been protected throughout my dreaming?

Yes. We will not let you destroy yourself. Your reality cannot *be* destroyed because what God creates is eternal. You can pretend to die in as many lifetimes as you choose, as you can pretend to be harmed, and do harm, as much as you like within each dream lifetime. But not forever. Eternity is eternally patient, but timelines always come to an end, in time.

You are concerned because you believe you have not always been so well protected. You have blundered into some painful situations that you feel could have been easily avoided with proper guidance. It would be difficult for you to now recall what guidance you had *asked for* preceding and during those situations.

The guidance you ask for always depends on who, and what, you think you are in the moment. If you believe you are a totally separate individual within a world of separation, you will be guided by ego thoughts of survival. They will usually be accompanied by feelings of fear, expressed as attack and defense, and the outcome of the situation will be judged by you from your point of view only. Great success might be experienced as feelings of grandiosity, which will usually be short lived, as they become hollow. Great failure will lead to feelings of despair, depression, and the sensation that you are absolutely and completely alone.

If you believe in your heart that, at some level, the essence of you is connected to the essence of all of humanity, within a foundation of communication, equality, and love, then you will feel your own loving presence. You will know what you are. It is from this place that you will seek guidance. And you will receive it. And as impossible as it may seem, the guidance will be such that everyone will gain and no one will lose. You will experience peace with no trace of fear.

So if you would seek protection during your remaining journey from illusion to reality, what are you to be protected *from*? And what is it that really requires protection? Nothing can harm you but your own thoughts. And your own thoughts can exist nowhere except in your own mind. Do not bother to think of anything more complicated than this within the realm of protection.

Your thoughts now immediately go to your body and the bodies of others. Surely they can be harmed and surely they need protection. It is neither necessary nor practical to deny the existence of bodies and their importance within the world you now see. All your body's senses tell you that the body is undeniable and real. Of course, those same senses tell you that the world you see is real. The split with reality arises when you perceive the body as being your *identity*, the essence of you. Your thoughts now leave no room for any other perception of reality, and you are stuck in time. The body ages and you appear to die.

If you can realize that the world you see is a projection of your thoughts, then it also becomes possible that the bodies you see within that world, including your own, are projections of your thoughts as well. What is a body? Do you have the same body you had twenty years ago? Have your *thoughts* about the body changed? How about when you were a child? Did you have the same thoughts and the same body then as you do now? It is only your thoughts *about* the body that cause it to appear to change. The body has no will of its own. This is essential to understand.

The real issue at hand is one of cause and effect. If your body created your life, then it must be in control of your life, and can actually dictate your wellbeing. It must be who you are, the cause of you. You have actually believed this. If your body died, then your life, your existence, would be over. How ridiculous this idea is. Your body created your mind, grew with it *as* it, and then died with it? Where did this tremendous power of creation come from? Where did it go?

Perhaps it is more realistic to believe that the mind has projected the body as it has projected the world and then, in pre-planned amnesia, got lost in both. This must have looked like a really fun game at the outset. It played hide and seek with itself and made all the props necessary to make it seem real.

And in the process it could play hide and seek with God.

You do not understand the power of your mind and the power of thought projected *by* mind. You do not understand it because you do not understand the power of God, Who created your eternal mind and endowed you with the power to use it, and the power to share it.

What needs protection? Only your thoughts about who, and what, you are, and your thoughts about who, and what, every living thing in creation is. For it is all joined, and it is all shared. It is all you, and it is all everyone. And it is all God.

For the moment, you have need to concern yourself only with your own mind, as you understand it. There is no need to worry about falling back asleep once you have awakened. Once you have totally awakened to your reality, the ideas of protection and dreaming will have no meaning. Yet for now, your thoughts are being protected by the guidance you seek. Ego thoughts are protected only by the idea of separation, and maintained by the fragment of your mind which chose to make it seem real.

Yet beneath its loud and empty commands, lies the light placed in your heart at your creation that can never be extinguished. Its protection ensures that ego thoughts of death and destruction are seen as the impossible nightmare they are. For the only thing that can die is the dream itself, when the mind returns to awareness of its wholeness. It is only from this place of light that guidance can be summoned and truly received, for here intention is sincere. Calls that benefit only the ego, that are disguised as calls to light, will be answered only by the ego.

Yet your true protection cannot fail and awaits only your heartfelt call. Here is thought aligned in mind with spirit. And here is the knowing that what is as one with everything, needs protection from nothing. And the guidance you seek will lead you to this awareness. For truth cannot fail to be true.

Christ Who Is Complete

Is one of my functions to provide entertainment?

Your real concern is that, as you stumble through your seemingly private world, you are being watched and laughed at by beings of higher realms, as if you are a witless clown. Not only would exposing what you thought was private be extremely painful and embarrassing to you, but you also believe that in the past you have mocked God, to the point of declaring the absence of His existence. You are somewhat in fear of retaliation because you have been unwilling to entirely let go of your belief that justice *requires* retaliation.

It should be made clear that God *cannot* be mocked, except in dream worlds of no reality. For God to be mocked by you, He would have to believe that what you now think you are is your reality, that the world you now think you are in is real, and that God's own Identity lies within the world you have made. None of these beliefs remain possible in reality.

Now that we can sense some relief within you, we can address your concerns that you are being watched and laughed at by what you deem to be higher beings. You do not consider this to be funny. In fact, it remains a trust factor for you. How could you trust the guidance of entities you believe might not be taking you seriously?

We can tell you that you have taken yourself so seriously that you have left nothing else for us to do except see the light side of you. And this we do. For we can find no darkness in the reality of you.

So now we can confide in you that we have found you not only funny, but also hilarious. You crack us up, so to speak. Have you ever watched videos of little puppies or kittens when they see themselves for the first time in a mirror? Some are frightened and attack, bumping noses with a much harder version of themselves. Some want to join, only to find the tongue of their newly discovered friend has little in common with their own. You have no idea of the endless enjoyment you have been providing for us. The jingle in your head that drives you crazy, the things you lose that show up in places you could not possibly have placed them. And don't even get us started on socks and washing machines. That is just the tip of the iceberg. The things you do when you think no one is looking have us in stitches.

It is when you are around others that the fun really begins. You are a riot. Did you know that we have been able to get you to break wind at the precise moment when you were least expecting it? I laughed so hard that I had to slap the back of the angel sitting next to me. My hand passed right through her wings and we both ended up on the floor just roaring. She said, "Where did this floor come from?" I said, "I have no idea. And where in hell did I get this hand?" That was too much for her and she split wide open. Angel dust everywhere. This one is still going around the halls of Heaven. She is just fine now, by the way.

Perhaps that answers your unstated wondering as to whether we guides have a sense of humor. Joy is what we do and who we are. Is it at your expense? How seriously do you take yourself and your world? Do you see your world as a reflection of yourself and want to join with others in friendship? Or do you see a fearful reflection that requires attack and defense? In neither case is what you see outside of you.

The puppy and the kitten eventually realize that the struggle to attack or join with what is not there, has no meaningful influence on what they are. Yet the *intention* to join always leads you a step closer to the awareness of your own reality. Through this intention to join, you will be guided to the awareness that you already *are* joined with every aspect of creation. It is here that you will experience the joy that is *always* shared by all.

Christ Who Is Complete

Is all the world a stage?

You are not a student of Shakespeare, but that these words have withstood the test of time in your world suggests that what they symbolize is meaningful. You are now being told the world you behold is a reflection and interpretation of what is in your limited mind, based upon the concept of an individual ego, or separateness of existence. You are also being told that the only reality is love expressed.

You are confused about your dream world, as are all dreamers. If the figures in your world are images you have made, you wonder how it can be that you can feel the love you express for some of them, and feel the love they express in return. This is very real to you. Does it not make *them* real? In a sense it does, for only love *is* real. But you do not see the wholeness of them, and they do not see the wholeness of you. This is because you are both appearing in your own personal dreams that connect in a "special" moment of love. Yet in this moment neither is defending a personal dream in a personal world. Both are sharing a common experience of expressing and receiving love. In that moment nothing else matters, including defense of each separate personality, if the feelings are real.

The fact that these feelings can, and do, fade, reflects the return of each to a respective dream world of personal reality. One or both may feel that they have let the other down, or they themselves have been let down. But they know that if the feeling is not there, then love is not there, in the moment. Again, neither has experienced the total wholeness of the other or the total wholeness of themselves, as evidenced by their respective return to personal identities in personal dream worlds. They have returned to what they still believe is their reality.

Expressed within your question is the idea that if the world is a stage, then characters performing, in order to interact in any meaningful way, must recognize the same set. They must experience the same stage. In other words, they must be in the same dream. Thus they must share responsibility for the dream. So if something goes wrong in the dream, they must share the blame. And since you have done things you regret within the dream but have not committed horrible crimes against humanity, the ones within the dream who have done so must accept the vast majority of the blame. Blame invites condemnation. Do you see the circle we have made and how your personal ego uses its own logic to project the guilt it experiences onto a world of its own making? This is quite a feat. But it is without accomplishment, for the ego mind's own thoughts of condemnation must remain within itself, having no world of reality to actually receive them.

Once again, the only way out of a dream is to stop dreaming. You are not an independent ego and your reality is not a dream. But since you still think it is, the only place we can reach you is within your own dream and at your own invitation. We reach you within the place you think you are hiding, when you finally recognize that the game is no longer that much fun, and you ask for help.

But we have still not answered your question in a satisfactory manner. Indeed you are not the only aspect of mind that believes it is sharing a stage. The prodigal son seems to be many, but in reality they are as one. Within the recognition of this oneness is love expressed. A stage is then no longer required, having been replaced by reality.

Yet no one on a journey of separation realizes he called forth the stage upon which his command performance is experienced. He embarked upon his grand adventure knowing the only way to make it seem real, and actually *be* an adventure, was total amnesia of the reality of oneness. Oneness itself could not exist in a world of separation. But you could not play alone. Other aspects of mind had to be willing to play their parts in your play, and for this you would play a part in theirs. Each would be a star in their own right and seek recognition as such from the others. And in order to play and make it real, each would forget reality. Yet reality never left them but merely waits.

So you agree on a general setting for a play. You call it a world. You think you see the same world, but you do not. You just assume you do. The only meaning in a world is your interpretation of it. From separate selves come separate interpretations and thus separate worlds. What each one sees is what is in the awareness of each at the moment. All the rest is non-existent to the separate self.

And within this strange group of characters you seek recognition. You believe their recognition of you might prove your own reality. Yes, the world you see is a stage. You have played many parts. You have seen your name in lights and you have found yourself cut from the cast. You have played the hero and the fool, the victim and the victimizer. You have laughed and cried and thought you have seen much of life. What you have seen are many dreams of separation, but within none have you found your freedom.

You do not have to keep choosing dreams. There is an alternative. You do not recognize the alternative because of your amnesia. But you realize the anesthetic is beginning to wear off, as the dreams appear to become more and more alike and less as adventures. Simply because you do not fully recognize an alternative does not mean that it is not there. But if you do not want it, you will not seek for it. And you will not ask for help in the seeking from a source that knows that dreams of separation are not real. The stage is set for your return, awaiting your call to truth.

Christ Who Is Complete

Am I not really alive within the world I see?

God is the giver of life. Life is love expressed. When love is not expressed, there is no life, and thus no awareness of God or Heaven. They are not gone, but what you think you are cannot find them. You ask this question because you have understood that there is no real life outside of Heaven. And you do believe you are outside of Heaven. Thus you must not really be alive.

In your personal dream world, you play the starring role and all others are supporting cast members. Most are there in your mind to help you prove your world is real, and you supply the same function for them. But a few are so important that you believe you could not live without them. These relationships you know as special, and they provide a basis for much of the love you express and receive. These are the ones with whom you can experience yourself as actually being alive.

Sometimes you love your work. You love your hobby or your sport. Sometimes you have a special love relationship with a pet. And just about anyone's baby if it is smiling and giggling. All of these situations make you feel alive and all involve an exchange of love to one degree or another. There is a direct relationship between feeling love and feeling that you are alive.

Most of the rest of the time you are struggling to *maintain* life in order to keep experiencing life, as you know it within your world. Here experiences are judged by you within a range from the mundane, to the threatening, to potentially terrifying. All these experiences and emotions combined could seem to represent a normal life to you. They could be summed up as love relationships, fear relationships, and those you do not care about, because they are basically out of mind.

Your world is a real world to you and within its boundaries you are experiencing life throughout. For most of your current life you believed there was no alternative to what you were experiencing with your physical senses. Your body was you and it told you what was going on within you and around you.

Now you are being told that all your experiences are experienced only within your mind, and you have projected the world you see onto a three-dimensional screen that seems to be outside of you. That others seem to have done the same and that they all appear to somewhat coordinate and interact, convinces all involved that it must be real. Within each projected world each can play the lead role, consider all others as supporting cast members, and develop their own special love relationships and special fear relationships. The adventure in separation is underway. The fact that there had to be some agreement among aspects of mind that chose to play the game of specialness and separation to begin with, is conveniently lost within the additional agreement of total amnesia.

Again, it is from this place, within the timeline of this adventure, from which you ask your question. Yet the fact that you have progressed to the point of asking it, means that you are willing to accept the possibility there are alternatives to the world you see and the life you live within it.

Once again, God gives life and life is love. God created you as life and love. This is your reality. Nothing can change it. What God creates is eternal. Life is eternal. Death is only real in dreams. And dreams are not reality.

The gift of Love is freedom. God created your mind with all the freedom of His own. All of God's creation is free to live and love and to be in direct relationship with every aspect of creation. None of this is done in dreams. This is reality. This is Heaven. Every relationship is a holy relationship. Yet none are special. For specialness excludes, and there is no exclusion in Heaven.

You can look for life in your dream world and you can look for Heaven there. But as long as you attempt to carve out a special little piece of eternity for yourself alone, including only a few others to help prove your reality and make the little kingdom you must protect more bearable, you will find neither Heaven nor peace nor freedom.

The dream world you have made, and your interpretation of all the people in it, as well as the self you think you made, are all prisoners within your own mind. You have the power to set them all free and to free yourself in the process. Then you will find that the Heaven you have been looking for is there within the Self you have denied.

And within this awakening, it will be as if you have never *really* lived at all within your dream.

Christ Who Is Complete

Am I in hell?

Your lack of religious experience has provided you with no coherent concept of what hell might be, and this is of benefit to you. For any concept of hell would have to be undone, along with the rest of your dream. Yet anything that is not the reality of Heaven could certainly appear to be experienced as hell.

Hell has been presented in your world as a fall from God's grace. You have been led to believe that the quest for the knowledge of good and evil led to all of humanity being expelled from paradise. This was apparently necessary in the name of justice and righteousness. You have seen vivid paintings by some of the great artists of their day attempting to portray the torture and the suffering of hell.

You cannot create a god of vengeance, except in your dream, no matter how many other dream figures seem to support the story and give it a life of its own. It is still *your* dream because it all exists within *your* mind. You can attempt to go about changing history as you know it, or you can change your mind about the reality of what you think you know. Which do you choose? For it is your choice.

The fact that you do not know your own identity coincides with the fact that you do not know God's. If a God of love somehow became a god of vengeance, then it would no longer be a God of love. It would have destroyed It's own reality and brought about an end to Itself. Do you really think this is possible *except* in a dream?

You hold on to the guilt that seems to make this story real. Without the guilt attached, there is only innocence. Then what vengeance is due? Who would punish the innocent, except those projecting their own guilt? To the guilty *no one* is innocent, for if guilt is real, it must be everywhere. Innocence itself then stands as a threat to this belief.

What is the knowledge of good and evil except the belief that some are innocent and some are guilty? Yet the truly innocent can see *no one* as guilty. And those who believe they are truly guilty cannot stomach the concept that anyone in their world could be truly innocent. This is the game that is being played in your dream world and it appears it has been played this way since time began. But time never begins at all except within dreams. And time ends where it began.

A dream world in which love is parceled out between a select few, while you fend off all that is kept outside waiting to pronounce justice upon you, would be hell. And if you think your world is real, then you will think that hell is real. And it will never change. Not until you change your mind about what you think you are.

There is no hell in Heaven, where your reality lies. It is beyond stories and dreams and time itself.

It has always been and will always be. It includes and does not exclude.

The nature of your healed mind is abstract. That is how it can *be* inclusive and maintain awareness of everything within its beingness. In its desire to play the game of specialness and separation, part of your mind became attached to a specific thought of a special you with special friends and special enemies, as required for drama, all set upon the backdrop of a world within which you wanted to play. That world sometimes seems pleasant and sometimes seems like hell, but you grow weary, for it has never fulfilled the promise you had hoped for. It never became paradise.

Yet even your world will be transformed, if you do not try to keep it to yourself alone. It will not be transformed *by* you, but it will be done with your permission and invitation. You will be a witness to your own awakening, and it will appear to happen within the flowering of a world you thought you knew, but have never really experienced. And Heaven on earth will appear to you through the Grace of God.

Christ Who Is Complete

What is abstract mind?

I can speak to you *about* abstract mind, but only abstract mind itself can fully comprehend the meaning behind the words.

The mind you use now, the one that you think is your whole mind, does not understand the abstract, all-inclusive Mind. This is because it is so focused on the story it made of a separate you in a separate world that it cannot seem to let it go. It does not *want* to let it go, because it thinks it created *you*. And, as long as you associate your identity with it, you will agree, and believe it is indeed you, and is your reality. This is what you have done. This is the game. And of course the amnesia built into the game means you have forgotten what you have done.

Even within the dream you can understand you are not aware of the workings of your greater mind as a whole. You associate your conscious mind with your self, your subconscious as a storehouse of information from past experience, or perhaps past lives, and your superconscious as inspiration, the higher self, or some other name that is meaningful to you. To these you can add the unconscious. You can realize you are not *consciously* connected to your whole mind as you gaze out upon your world.

For simplicity, let us say that one aspect of your whole mind attached itself to a thought. The thought might be, "What if everything was separate from everything, instead of connected in mind? What would that look like?" You see, as long as you looked at this with your whole mind, you would realize this is impossible, because everything exists within mind, and the whole mind *knows* it is connected to all minds and everything in God's creation.

So to continue our simple story, how could the impossible be made possible? Since only mind creates, one aspect of mind had to appear to attach itself to a specific thought to produce a specific story of separation. Minds cannot be separate in reality. Yet the minds that God creates are created to be free, as well as to know themselves as everything. Within this freedom of mind, the ability to pretend to be imprisoned was not denied. The impossible could appear to be made possible, if an aspect of mind could imagine itself to be split off from the whole and follow a thought by itself. This would only work if the aspect could *forget* that it is part of the whole mind. It had to pretend to fall asleep and feign amnesia.

Your whole mind is your abstract mind. It knows where you are and knows you are pretending. Yet everything God creates contains all of creation. This includes an aspect of mind pretending to be sleeping and split from the whole. What is created free, will not have freedom rescinded, even if that freedom is used for limitation and imprisonment within an illusion. Yet what is created eternal will always grow tired of imprisonment within time, as the adventure loses its luster.

Now you have opened the door, ever so slightly. You have asked for help. It is your sleeping mind itself that is beginning to stir from slumber, drowsily wondering where it is and how it got there. It did a wonderful job with the amnesia. It needs to be told what it is.

The abstract Mind of God encompasses all that is, because It *is* All That Is. What God creates cannot be less than Itself or God would have created separation and caused Its own destruction by dividing Itself into pieces, each less than all that is. So what God creates in each is an aspect of the Whole perfectly connected to every other aspect of the Whole. Do you see the holographic nature? Everything God creates knows its Identity in God as one with All That Is. Everything in creation *shares* the abstract Mind of God. Thus is the One, or Whole, Son of God expressed through infinite extensions of God that become known collectively as the Sonship.

Your mind is as abstract as God's because it *is* God's in reality. This is why you cannot change it to become less than what you are. Yet God gave you freedom as an attribute of your creation, and an aspect of your mind attached itself to a thought of separation. This aspect of mind therefore became focused on the specific, to the exclusion of everything else. It became concrete, rather than abstract in nature. It remains stuck in the concrete.

A timeline of illusion, or specific story of separation, was constructed.

This is only a belief by a fragment of your mind. Your whole abstract Self allows it to play make believe, knowing it is in no danger. When it *really* wants to leave the dream, the means has already been provided. This God Himself has assured with the creation of the Holy Spirit.

Christ Who Is Complete

What is the difference between my normal dream
world and my dreams at night?

Both lack substance in reality, but within
your present experience, they represent alternate
states of mind. The consciousness you experience in
your waking world directs you to be primarily self-
aware. In your sleep, that consciousness is relaxed,
allowing other aspects of mind to be present that
had been blocked by your consciousness during
much of the waking day.

Your overall belief system is represented in
both states of mind and is very relevant to what
appears in your sleeping dreams, as well as in
consciousness. This is why what is in your
consciousness directly before falling asleep
significantly influences the nature of your dreaming.
All those in dream worlds of their own making also
dream in sleep, but memory is selective. Many
revelations and discoveries in your world were
received from guidance within the sleep state, when
the complexities and misdirection of the conscious
mind were temporarily set aside.

Guidance is always available to you, as is all
of reality. It is limited only by your unwillingness to
hear and by your desire to focus instead on specifics
within your personal world. As is always the case,
the matter may be condensed into simple questions.

What do you want? What do you value? What is important to you? Your mind is always a servant of your desires. When you do not know what you want, your mind will reflect the confusion. This will be true in consciousness as well as the sleep state.

The whole purpose of our communication is to help you establish what you *do* want. You have opened the door because you have found your world wanting. All aspects of mind work amazingly well together, when you are totally clear as to the goal you would achieve. Does your goal still reside within the personal world of your making? Is this where you would establish your purpose?

You are still looking for your purpose, because alternatives to your world seem remote and fuzzy in focus. The idea of all encompassing love seems itself an unattainable dream. You cannot choose what you cannot accept as possible.

Whether you have pleasant dreams or nightmares depends on what you think you are and what your purpose is. We can tell you that your identity is love itself, and your purpose is to extend that love. But without your belief in the truth of these words, they will have no effect on your dreams or your waking from them.

You have taken an important step. When you finally realize your world is a dream, you will also recognize how easily it can be changed, for you have been shown this in your sleeping dreams. Then you will find that all the baggage you believe you have accumulated over the years will be simply left behind in the dream that was never real. In addition, all the guilt that you have held within, or projected outward, will vanish in the same instant of awakening.

Are you ready to let all this go? This question will lead you to discover what you still value and would grasp tightly in fear of loss. Perhaps it would be guilt itself. For this belief is deep-seated and highly prized. It is important that you look closely at what you value, that you may find where the value actually lies within it.

You have not sinned, nor has anyone sinned against you, except in your dream. Within it are bodies real, and attack and defense justified and hailed, with all manner of terror forcing itself onto center stage. What would you retain from your dream except loving moments shared? What else has value?

We are here to tell you that these loving moments are already saved and kept for you. Yet they represent only a minute fragment of the wholeness of you. We offer our guidance to you toward the remembrance of the fullness of your Self that resides beyond dreams.

Christ Who Is Complete

Can a person fundamentally change within one
lifetime without experiencing
a major disaster?

There are many facets to your question.
First, you accept that there can be fundamental
change as a result of a disaster experience. This
person's external world is already fundamentally
changed by disaster. So it is likely the internal
world, or mind, will be changed as well. A
reevaluation of what is of value will appear to have
been forced upon this individual.

By now you may realize that there could *be*
no disaster in this person's world that was not first
called forth to be experienced within a "personal"
mind. The fact that others wished to experience
similar circumstances within their own minds is
what brought about the projection of the disaster in
their respective outer worlds. Without the
understanding of this cause and effect, no further
explanations will be meaningful to you. So you must
understand that this person had already *decided* to
change at some level within mind, with the belief
that such an occurrence would help facilitate the
change.

This goes to the heart of your question. You
wonder if there is a kinder, gentler way to
experience transformation, and still have the

process completed within one lifetime. You perceive, not totally incorrectly, that one aspect of your mind is attempting to break through a barrier to reach another aspect of your mind and, without this achievement, more drastic measures will be used to get your attention. This makes you wonder if you actually have paid your dues, or if there is more to pay.

You do not owe anything except to yourself. You owe yourself a way out of the dream that you believe you are trapped within. You search for escape from a self-imposed amnesia. You have reinforced the barricades you perceive through many years of projecting judgments of blame and guilt and condemnation onto a world that could not hold them, because it was not real. So they return to you who is their source.

You will change. You will change back to your changeless reality. There is no question of this. Within your world there is no permanency, despite all efforts to make it so. Yet all these changes will be cosmetic. You can change one dream for another that promises to be more appealing. You can even appear to end one dream and begin another, with hopes of a happier outcome. How can any dream have a happy outcome if one of its requirements is a belief in death?

Would you choose a smoother transition and avoid disaster? Become as a little child. Little children do not know what anything is for. They are willing to be taught. They do not enter into an experience presuming they already understand what value lies within it and how it will progress. They carry an innocence of perception and an absence of baggage. And above all, with the proper guidance, they always feel that they are safe.

Your reality is safe. It has always been so and will always be so. You cannot change this, even with all the power and fury of your dreams of disaster. You cannot become what you were not created to be. And you cannot create the reality of yourself within a dream.

You have already decided to change, or you would not be open to receiving these words. Your decision will bring the required outcome. You do not have to attempt to manufacture the outcome from within your dream. It cannot be done. The help you receive comes not from within your dream of separation but from the wholeness of your Self. This Self includes all that God created, and nothing else. Because there is nothing else. And nothing that God created can be separated from anything God created.

Find peace in knowing you cannot be separated from your Self. Find comfort in knowing the path to your remembering will not be constructed by a dream figure in a dream. Find the happiness of a child who understands the way home may not be clear, but the surety of the outcome is guaranteed by One Who can give only love. And this you cannot change.

Christic Who Is Complete

Why is separation impossible?

Separation is impossible in the sense that total separation would be meaningless.

Separation appears very real to you because it is all you seem to experience in your physical world. This is a projection of the original thought that separation indeed is possible, and the world you see is the proof required. Yet illusion of separation is not separation. Every aspect of the world you see is connected to every other aspect because the images were all established by *your* mind within *your* dream. Your entire dream represents the oneness of them. Where are all the separate pieces of your dreams at night when you awaken in the morning?

Your dream world is one complete interconnected series of experiences you call the story of your life. It is based upon experiencing nearly countless interactions with other seemingly separate people, life forms, and forms in general. These forms have no life, except within the minds that generated the thoughts that projected the forms onto the screen. Forms have no lives of their own. They only symbolize the life of the mind, which projected them into form through very focused, and restricted thought patterns.

You are all good at what you do. You have made your dreams of separation seem real. We have already stated that minds choosing the game of separation must be in agreement at the outset of the timeline, in order to appear to play on the same stage. There is no real separation. But the stories of separation are legion and limited only by the minds that make them. Which means they are not limited at all. Neither are they limited in reality, because they never existed in reality.

The thought of separation is an idea. Let us take this idea to its logical conclusion, even within your world of separation. If separation is possible, *total* separation must be possible. Let us look at a separate you, the you represented by the body that you think you are. Now let us take this separate you into your separate world. But wait. We already have a problem. We cannot *have* a totally separate you if we are taking your world along. So here we now have you, alone, a separate body in space. No stars, because you are totally separate. What would you like to do now? Perhaps you could look at your hand. But there would be no light to see it by. You could feel it with your other hand. But then you realize you cannot have two hands in separation. One of them must go. Then it occurs to you that all your body parts are connected to each other. This must be dismantled down to the individual cells. But cells are a collection of molecules, and molecules a collection of atoms, and atoms consist of subatomic particles. You have disappeared within total separation.

Do you see that *nothing* can exist in total separation? Nothing can in form, and nothing can in mind. Connection of everything to everything is innate. The innateness of the connection of everything to everything is what allows meaning to exist for *anything* within everything. There is a simple word symbol that represents the idea of this connection of everything to everything. It is called love. It could be called totality. It could be called reality. It could be called God. It could be called you.

Christ Who Is Complete

What is this voice of self-condemnation I often hear?

You do not hear it as often as you used to. Recently, when you have remembered, you have been turning it over to the Holy Spirit. Now you wonder if you should be turning it over to me.

This voice of condemnation has a source that believes it is imprisoned, and being too limited to recognize what caused its apparent imprisonment, it will project blame to all entities which would receive it. The aspect of your mind that wished to embark on its personal grand adventure chose a story of triumph, heroism, and above all specialness. Another name for this is the ego mind. The ego mind, which you seem to experience as yourself, represents a small deluded fragment of your whole mind, which has set off on a journey of its own making.

This fragment of mind thinks that it has created you as the central character in *its* story. When you agree with it and accept that this is what you really are, in effect, you believe you have created yourself within the story of your *own* world. If you created yourself, then God could not have created you as an extension of all of creation. You are now alone within a story about a separate you navigating a world of countless other beings, entities, and objects which apparently have no intrinsic connection to one another.

You have entered a world of fear. And this takes place in your mind, where all relationships are experienced. The character you have willingly played seems to have been born into a body, for the story needs a suitable beginning, as it needs a suitable end. The seamlessness of the transition, or aging, of the body over the "life" of the story, keeps you from wondering how you could actually *be* a body. But you *have* believed you are a body within a world not of your own making.

As we have said, this fragment of your mind that seemed to project the story of you had to forget that it was an aspect of the whole mind, in order to make a story of separation seem real. Otherwise the story would have ended at its beginning, with the realization that the idea of totally separate entities is impossible. This fragment of mind had to forget what it *really* is in order to pretend to *become* you, the character you now seem to be playing.

There are a few problems with this make believe situation. You have not been a very good hero. You have not turned out to be as special as your would-be creator had hoped for. And your body, which was required in order that you appear to be separate, was a far too limited and pitiful kingdom for this self-made ruler to reign within. *You* must have let it down, for surely *it* was not at fault. When it started on this adventure, it looked as if it had created a wonderful and special identity.

The fact that no aspect of creation can be more or less valuable or special than any other aspect of creation was forgotten with the making of the story.

But a story without a foundation in reality will eventually be disclosed as a story without meaning. One which always ends in death. Stories without meaning become stories that lose support over time. Stories of darkness require support to keep the door closed against the light. A small crack in the door would reveal a shaft of light, which would prove the darkness itself was not real.

The maker of this personal and special chamber, built to escape the light, no longer remembers its own reality. It has forgotten that it *is* the light. It believes the light would attack it and destroy it. So it will defend with its "life" its self-made chamber of isolation, and its personal world of separation.

You are what this mistaken aspect of mind fears. And fear it does. For by making a story seem real that always ends in death, it has made fear real for itself. Fear exists *nowhere* except in stories of death. Fear requires escape or attack. There are no other choices, except death. When light begins to enter the ego mind's chamber of darkness, the ego knows it cannot escape, for there is nowhere to go. So it must attack. It must attack you.

For *you* are what has invited in the light. You are carefully and cautiously beginning to open the door. You are beginning to awaken. The ego mind is familiar with irony, but totally blind to the glaring magnitude of the irony at hand. What it believes would totally obliterate every aspect of itself and its story, is the only thing that can save any part of both. What but the whole mind can save any aspect of itself from attachment to an impossible thought? *You* are the whole mind. What should be saved within a story except that which has meaning? And what has meaning that is not love? Yet should a dreamer be condemned who within his dream has forgotten his reality?

It is you who are the only hope of salvation for this lost and fearful fragment of mind that would condemn you. You are still sleepy and still stumble in the dim light, but there is no turning back on the path you have now chosen. It is becoming clearer that there is nothing of value to turn back to that will not be saved and awaiting you at your destination.

Listen again to this voice of self-condemnation and know the self it would condemn is not you, but a fictional hero in a fictional story. Perhaps you can hear, in place of condemnation, a desperate call for help from a fearful child whose dream turned into a nightmare. The child may even strike out in its sleep, but there will be nothing to hit but pillows and blankets. Upon awakening, you will be there. And you will embrace the child. And you will know you are as one, because reality cannot be separated by a dream.

The impossible journey, and all the condemnation and horror that seemed to make the nightmare so real, will have ended in time, where they began. And they will have had no effect upon reality, except the lingering effects of all the moments of love expressed within the dream.

Christ Who Is Complete

What is the Living God?

You are somewhat fearful to ask this question, because you believe you are already supposed to know the answer based upon your past spiritual learning. You are also concerned that this question has been asked throughout time, and mankind has yet to come to agreement on any meaningful definition, due to individual beliefs, cultures, and traditions.

Of note within your question is the word, living. You seek to experience a God Who is no longer theoretical, but practical and real. A theoretical god is useful only in theoretical situations, and your belief in such a god is likely to be theoretical as well. If God is real, this is the God you wish to connect with and understand.

There is a school of thought which promotes the idea that God is impossible to know and understand, and is by nature always to be the "Great Mystery." Surely it must be clear that if God wished to forever remain a mystery to you, then He would also have decided to remain forever separate from you. Is this a God of love and unity of purpose? How can you embrace a mystery?

So if God Himself wishes to be known and understood by you, because you are joined *in* Him, what is keeping this from your present awareness?

Tradition would answer that you have been cast out of Heaven for your sinful ways. In fact, you were already cast out of Heaven when you were born, because these sinful ways go all the way back to Adam and Eve. Humanity must still suffer from original sin until a proper savior is found. Christ represents salvation for some, but not for all, within your world.

Now we are back to where we always must return. We have returned to the world in your mind, as you believe it to be. Once more, there is nowhere else to go in order to actually address your question. If you are going to find the Living God, where do you think you might begin to look? Why do you think you have not seriously looked there before?

It is because you are afraid that you might actually *find* God there. Then where would your world be? What would the reality of your world look like if exposed to the Light of Everything? The fear of God has been hiding within the ego mind of separation ever since the inception of the dream. How could it be otherwise? Full, sudden exposure of the illusion to all of creation at once could only result in terror for the fragment of mind lost in its own world, still believing it is the *whole* world. To whatever extent you believe you *are* this ego mind, to that same extent will that terror appear to be yours.

This is why you cannot be rudely awakened from the dream all at once. It is still too real for you and you still highly value more of it than you realize.

Yet this world itself will begin to change as you gradually let more light in and become accustomed to it. As you seek for more light, it will appear. As your desire for peace increases, it is more peace that you will find. Your world will actually change. This is true because you will always see what your mind has projected out onto the stage. And what it projects is based on what it believes. And what it believes is determined by what it thinks it *is*.

If the mind thinks it is separate, it will find proof within its own dream, for that is why it was established. If the mind begins to understand that everything is connected, it will also find proof it is so, for it is beginning to allow reality to return. This proof will be experienced as more peace and joy and love. There will be more lightness of being and less heaviness of existence. There will be less struggle and more ease. And when struggle does appear, you will realize it is because you have discovered within yourself a strong attachment to valuing something within your dream.

A Living God is One Who expresses Itself through all of creation. It is a living representation of everything *in* creation. It is an awareness of all aspects of creation being alive within Itself and Itself being alive in all aspects of creation. It is abstract awareness of a totality that excludes nothing, because love is all encompassing.

It is your own reality. For your reality is the light of the Living God expressing Itself as you.

Christuf Who Is Complete

Why have I always felt the need to be right?

It is because you never wanted to be wrong. And you thought that, basically, these were the only two alternatives available to you in your world of polarity. It is similar to your adventure into the search for good and evil. In order to find either, you had to believe *both* were real and available to be discovered. The idea of seek and you will find will eventually be fruitful to the mind which projects what it *wishes* to see upon the world it has chosen for that very purpose.

Your need to be right has a root cause. But the real question is, "Who is the you that feels it must be right?" The you of the dream who asks this question has two basic functions. You must defend your dream, and you must fortify the reality of your position within it. If you are wrong, then your belief system may be wrong. If your belief system is wrong, then your dream might not be real.

The idea of right and wrong establishes the concept of separation at the outset. Having to choose between two things implies that they are already separate, and it is up to you to choose which is which. Within the dream, that choice is always made with regard to what is good for the personal you, and what is not. Anything that does not fall into one of those two categories is considered irrelevant and meaningless, within your personal dream world. These things are merely background noise or part of the stage setting. You do not notice them because you did not project them into your story.

You do not realize how your search for right and wrong, based upon personal gain, automatically requires you to judge everything and everyone you interact with accordingly. The default position of your belief system thus *requires* judgment in order to find out what is good for the personal you. This judgment is not natural to your reality, which judges nothing but interacts with everything. This apparent conflict, which does not exist in reality, results in unconscious stress and significant hidden guilt within your dream. Something deep within you knows that when you use judgment to single out specialness in your personal favor, you are not being true to your own reality. This is true despite the fact that you appear to be unconscious *to* your own reality.

This explains why, when you go out of your way to prove you are right in a situation, even if everyone should come to that agreement, you still do not feel good about yourself for any appreciable length of time. There is no thrill of victory when you discover there was no contest in the first place. A discussion can have no winner or loser in reality, just a sharing. Being right means you want to take credit for something that belongs to the universe and force it to belong to the personal you.

You have no need to be right and you have no need to be wrong. You do have a need to awaken to your own reality. And you can use your expertise at judgment to help you do so. This requires a change in direction, a change in purpose, and a change in the meaning of the word judgment itself.

What if aspects of reality have been very close to you on your journey, but you have missed them all along? Perhaps you could change your purpose from wanting to be right for the benefit of a personal you, to a search for aspects of reality, even within your own personal dream. This could be a fun game. Especially if you could leave behind the guilt you have been dragging along with you from your previous purposes and goals.

First, let us change the word judgment to the word discernment. You need judge nothing. But you *are* required to discern between what truth is and what illusion is within your dream. Yes, we have told you there are aspects of truth even there. They are moments of love expressed. You believe they have been relatively few, and you have had some difficulty identifying them. This is for a very simple reason. You have not been looking for them. You have been too busy defending your dream world and fortifying your identity within it. You have been so entrenched in this purpose and this way of looking, that you need a guide to help you see differently.

What you see in all things in your world is based upon what you *want* to see there. All else is overlooked. If your purpose becomes to seek for moments of love expressed, you will be amazed at how much love you experience that you never thought was there. You will eventually find that it can be no other way.

Do not bother to search for your reality in a world of strife and suffering, for it cannot be found there. And be glad it is not up to you to judge what is right or wrong, or good or evil. You are a poor judge, with an extremely narrow point of view. Be glad as well that, when you have changed your purpose, a Guide Who can discern between what reflects truth and what is illusion in *all* dreams, is available to you upon your honest request, made free of the parameters you would establish from within the dream. He knows your reality, as does all of reality outside of your dream. And He will always lead you on a path that is the right one for you.

Christ Who Is Complete

How many parts have I played within the dream?

There are overtones to your question beyond the obvious issue of reincarnation. You question whether your current life, or any previous ones, have had any real meaning, or if you have been merely playing characters in some gigantic absurd play.

It is important for you to understand that we are here neither to attack your belief system nor your world. We are here at your invitation, because you are beginning to lose faith in both. As in all things, you will find some meaning within your belief system, where you seek for it. Whether you experience *real* meaning depends on the nature of love expressed.

Within eternity, all timelines have already begun and expired. All stories that seemed to contain a past and a future are contained within timelessness, and can only be experienced in completion within the eternal now. This includes all aspects of mind which would dream, and all the dreams they would compose. You are free to explore past dreams and reincarnated selves, and plan for future ones in a better story. They are all ended and complete, and they are all yet to begin. From which point of reference would you wish to experience them? Perhaps some point in between. Maybe from within one of the stories.

You are beginning to realize you do not have to play every part in every play, seeking for love outside yourself. Yet the distance from your current belief system to the unity of abstract Mind appears too great to be traversed within a single awakening. The sudden explosion of comprehension would overwhelm the fragment of mind that still holds on to some hope of reality for its special world and special characters and special self.

You are changing and you are beginning to recognize that there must be something more that you have been missing. It would be *yourself* that now must have compassion for this aspect of mind lost in its own dreams. For you are no longer its main character. You are separating yourself from *its* story of separation from the whole. You can no longer pretend to be completely asleep within a story over which you have no control. And you are no longer a victim within it.

So what of this lost aspect of mind? Shall we condemn it because it has sinned, and ban it forever from the wholeness of Mind? What has it really done? It has attached itself to an impossible thought and allowed itself to be carried away. It got lost in the idea of separation, which, if carried to completion, would have resulted in its own extinction. The thought is simply what it is. It is the mind that must be healed. And banishment is not healing, but oblivion. It is also a concept unknown to the inclusiveness of wholeness.

You represent the savior of this aspect of mind, because it is an aspect of *your* wholeness. You are not complete without it, but you realize you no longer need its stories of heroes and villains and specialness. You may not be totally awakened but you now comprehend that you have the power to change the stories. The idea of separation no longer dictates what they must be, and that they must all end in death. And the stranglehold of guilt that accompanies them vanishes the instant it is clearly understood that mistakes are not sins, and thoughts can be set free by the mind that holds them.

What would you like your story to be? For you can easily change the one you are now experiencing. What would you seek for within it? Your mind will reflect its allegiance to the thoughts it wishes to be true, upon a screen that will appear as your world.

Perhaps it is time to return to playing the part of your one Self, as created within the Mind of God. It excludes no part of reality.

Christ Who Is Complete

What is freedom?

No one who knows what freedom is can believe it could be experienced from within a body, for the purpose of a body was to restrict, limit, and contain. It represents the ultimate "proof" that separation is real, and has been attained. Yet for those who believe in separation and specialness, the body seems to represent the only thing that can be free. The mind must be within it, and is identified as an organ called the brain. So the whole entity is born, lives, and dies, and freedom can only be experienced in that in between time called, life.

Freedom can be experienced in the only place that anything can be experienced, and that is within the mind of the one who experiences. Imprisonment of the body represents imprisonment of itself only to the mind which believes its identity *is* a body. There appears to be no way out of this situation unless the body is set free. The mind does not realize that it has already imprisoned *itself* within a body and it is *itself* that must be set free.

The body was required for the mind to believe itself to be the main character in a story of separation. It had to appear unique and separate from others who were required to have their own bodies. Within the dream you cannot tell the players without the bodies. And none of them represent freedom, because they are all imprisoned within the story. Who could possibly hold them all prisoners? It can only be the one who dreams the dream and *maintains* it.

You will never escape the dream you made unless you take responsibility as its maker. Only in this way can you take back control of the dream and have the ability to simply let it go. You built a prison you thought was paradise, locked yourself within, and gave the key to one who would be ruler. Then you took the "identity" of this ruler as your own, forgot your reality, and became the main character in a play you forgot you scripted.

Now you ask for freedom, and we answer. Yet we must reach you where you believe your reality is. We must reach you within the story you projected. And so we do. We enter your dream at your invitation. We can assure you that we will not become lost in it with you, because our purpose is simply to help you escape. It does not fascinate us. We have been waiting for your call, from outside of time.

You are *not* the character in your play. You are the actor who got so caught up in playing the part that he *became* the part, and fell asleep to his real identity. Now we have a strange situation. The call for help seems to come from the character in the play, but the *real* call is from the sleeping actor who is beginning to awaken and wonders what is going on. He does not yet realize he must *separate* himself from the character he has been playing, before he can really hear, and understand, the answer to his call.

We cannot explain what freedom is to a dreamer, because freedom lies outside the imprisonment of dreams. Freedom is a feeling and a knowing. Yet perhaps you can remember moments when you felt free, even within the dream. Perhaps they were moments when you felt so much love, that the concept of bodies was irrelevant.

PART II

Voice For God

What is my question?

We thought you would never ask. It has been some time since your last question. At that time you experienced some difficulty in receiving, and recording, the answers you received. They did not flow as well as earlier ones. You recognized your own resistance within this process, and felt it would be prudent to take a break so that clarity would not be sacrificed.

The fact that you identified the source of some of your resistance is evidenced by your current choice of words for guidance. Voice for God is, in your mind, somewhat less threatening than, Christ Who is complete. That your chosen source for guidance can be perceived as threatening at all, reveals only a hint of the fear of God you still retain in your mind. You have not yet escaped the projection of this fear onto whatever guide you choose to call upon and hear.

Let us go to the source of your fear. We know that it involves the perceived loss of your entire dream world, as well as your seeming existence within it. But we can be more specific than this within your current uneasiness. You believe there still must be some final test that you must take, and pass. This test would seem to require a tremendous amount of courage and faith, which you believe you do not now possess. Surely this test must be for someone else, and not you. You still cannot accept the idea of Christ, without accepting the idea of a required final test of crucifixion, or worse, many such tests.

We have told you that we will not tear you from your dream, but will help you release it as gently as you will allow. We have also told you that how much terror you experience is directly related to how much you value your world, and believe it to be your reality. And it is *this* that you fear. You realize you *do* value your world and do *not* want to let it go entirely. At this point within time, you simply cannot accept that the world you see, and the life you think you are living, are nothing more than the dream of an adventure gone bad, from which you can awaken entirely. You still do not know what you would awaken *to,* and still cannot comprehend a reality in which all is lovingly shared by all, and bodies are merely costumes worn in theatrical productions that can be set aside when not in use.

You are beginning to comprehend the power of your own mind, whether in dreams or reality, and that power is fearful to you, because you feel you can misuse it, as you have apparently done to put yourself in your current situation. This is why it is important to align the power of your mind with One Who knows how to use it only for benevolent healing and sharing of love.

The idea of aligning your mind with divine Guidance in every situation or thought process you encounter falls for you somewhere between highly unlikely and impossible. For your ego mind the latter will apply. We have said there is a you behind the ego that is beginning to awaken to the fact that the ego thought of separation is not your identity. You do have a real desire to see things differently. When that desire becomes what you really *want,* your default, or beginning position, will be with divine Guidance, and not the ego mind. In practical terms, you will greet each situation or thought process from a base of curiosity and acceptance, rather than one of wariness and separation.

Once again, the issue becomes one of trust and faith. And once again, this will be evidenced in the world you see as an expression of what you really *want.* For we have stated that you will find what you seek, depending upon the guide you choose. Do you really want peace, acceptance, joining, and healing, or do you want them only if it does not cost you your individual, self-proclaimed identity and specialness? Perhaps you would receive them sometimes, as long as you retain your right to reject them as you see fit, depending on particular circumstances. How would this work in the long run? You need only look at your life to this point for the answer.

We cannot remove fear from your mind, and leave you comfortably within a dream of unreality. Fear *attests* to the fact that your dream is not real. As you awaken from the amnesia, you will begin to comprehend that you are *choosing* fear over peace, in order to hang on to the remnants of your dream. Fear may be a thrill and somewhat exciting, but not when it turns to terror.

You need no test or crucifixion. What you desire will be reflected back to you from within your own dream. It is this you do not want to believe, and it is this that you believe will be tested. You still want the responsibility of your dream to fall outside of you who dream it. You still want to believe this is being done *to* you, against your will. If your whole Self is aware of your dream and allows a part of Its own mind to appear to suffer within It, you even consider yourself a victim of your Self.

You do not understand the importance of your *wanting* to leave your own dream. If you are not responsible for it, then you are at the mercy of it, with no control over the ability to leave. Then someone else dreamed *your* dream from which you cannot escape, unless this someone else so wills or whims.

You *can* choose to leave your own dream. *Know* this. And then know that there is a Guide Who will help you leave what you forgot you made.

Voice For God

Why have I done this to myself?

Your mind is not really open to receiving a clear answer to this question, since you have long asked it and already provided yourself with many possibilities as to why you find yourself where you believe you are.

We can review some of the thoughts you already have in your mind. First, and most obvious to you, is that you are playing the role you perceive simply because it is a possibility. If God is all encompassing, then all possibilities must be included, which cannot exclude yourself. Now you are being told that you and your world exist in a dream of separation, and reality is represented only by loving thoughts exchanged.

This led you to your next question. Why choose the dream in the first place? We have stated that those who dream of separation would be special and have their own tiny kingdoms of exclusion, which they would maintain till death as real, and somehow worth the tremendous effort to support. This fragment of mind would claim it is all that is, and *make* itself real within its own dream in time. Even the role of victim has appeal, as long as it can be yours alone and you can be the martyr in an unjust world.

This you now understand, and can accept to a degree, but you believe there must be more. If you were created in Heaven, why leave Heaven? Was Heaven not special enough, even if it is to be shared by all? Something does not add up within your current mindset.

You read one possible explanation some time ago that still appeals to you. God created each soul as all knowing, but each soul had to *experience* everything before becoming all being. That experiencing would have to include not only all that God is, but also all that God appears *not* to be. But what can God not be? God is all-inclusive and shares all with all. What it appears God cannot be, is *not* God. God cannot be *not* all-inclusive. A partial, all-inclusive God is meaningless.

Hence you seem to find yourself within a game of hide and seek with God. And you feel that this game is perhaps necessary so you may experience what God is not. As the prodigal son left home looking for something more, but finding only less, you feel it may have been your duty to experience something less than Heaven, so that you might more fully appreciated Heaven upon your return.

But here a potential problem arises. If God's plan for you were to leave reality in order to appreciate reality, it would seem that God is promoting sacrifice. For, if it were possible, leaving reality would be the ultimate sacrifice. It would *be* death. Yet leaving reality is *not* possible, nor is death. In your freedom, God *did* allow the dream of separation. And this you have accomplished, because it was your wish. And it still is. Yet you grow weary of looking for a personal heaven outside of Heaven. Who would you truly *share* it with? How much of what you perceive as not God would you need to experience before it would be enough? Perhaps the journey, if not seen to be in vain, can at least be recognized as accomplished.

Another possibility you have entertained is one in which a simple question was asked. "Is there anything other than Heaven?" The answer might have been that there cannot be more than everything in loving communion with everything. To this response you might have asked, "Can there be less?" And you were perhaps told that this was impossible. Then you may have wished the impossible to be possible out of innocent curiosity. Thus you could be absolved of the deep-seated, hidden guilt for having wanted your own special, separate kingdom and for the usurpation of God's power. Left unexplained is why you would remain in such a state if you *knew* it was a simple mistake and you were not guilty.

We have stated we are not here to remove from your mind thoughts and concepts that you are not yet ready to release. Nor are we here to support partial truths you may hold, and thereby solidify them more deeply within your current belief system. When you are ready to let *all* your thoughts and concepts be released, and come as a child innocent of perception, you will be led to the remembrance of your Self and recognize what has always been, and what will always be.

You are guilty only of dreaming. Dreaming is not a punishable offense. You *cannot* attack God and have not done so. Dreams always end in time, where they begin. Your final dream will be a happy one, in which everything will have been forgiven. You will experience this forgiveness and recognize that it comes from your Self *to* yourself, for you will be separate from nothing.

We will share a thought to perhaps help you with this matter. There is no darkness so dark that Light cannot enter. And when the Light has entered, then where is the darkness?

Voice For God

How many versions of me are there?

There is one version of you, and that is the one that God created. God creates by extending what God is. That is you. You are an extension of God, as is everything God creates. And what God created *is* everything. Nothing can be added to or removed from what God creates. Nothing can be added to or removed from your reality.

Your question, of course, is from within the dream. You have heard of parallel universes and parallel lives. You have read of split versions of yourself, let us say twelve, which are all living incomplete lives, and will join at some point to become super human, evidenced by many more strands of DNA. You will be able to manifest physical items at will. You will be able to do magic. We have told you that you already have done magic, by making a dream world and a dream identity.

Now we must ask some questions. Is this what has been missing from your life? What will you manifest first? Will what you manifest complete you and bring you peace? For how long?

And now a few more questions. How badly do you want parallel lives? You have been denied nothing, including your dream of separation. Perhaps you can finally make it better. How about a kingdom with a castle and a thousand servants? You would need no goose that lays golden eggs, for you could manifest all the riches you could desire. Now make your power unchallenged, so all would quake at the sound of your name, and bow low before your presence. Perhaps this is where the happiness that has eluded you lies.

Yet more questions. Who will love you? Thousands may proclaim their love for you and even worship you out of fear. Who will love you? Will you be able to manifest love as you manifest a beautiful jewel to look upon? How will you care for your worshipers? What will they be thinking and saying behind your back?

Perhaps they will be able to manifest too. Surely some of them would choose kingdoms. On one small planet conflicts must arise. The one who could manifest the greatest armies and most destructive weapons might win. If the planet survives. Maybe each could manifest a separate planet. But then would not one choose to be the most powerful king, with interplanetary warfare the ultimate result? Perhaps this has a familiar tone, of gods at war in the heavens.

We always come back to the same question. What is it that you really *want?* Do you believe there is a substitute for love? Perhaps it can be found in a parallel life. Perhaps it can be found in this one. Perhaps love is what you *are.* You can search as long as you choose, endeavoring to find the best vantage point from which to awaken from the dream.

Voice For God

How many Sons of God are there?

You are concerned with the loss of your identity. We have helped clarify the lack of reality in the world as you see it now, but what will replace it still is not clear enough to make you desire it above all else. You would like a picture of what your newly discovered Self might look like. You want to know how It lives and what It interacts with. The idea of oneness makes little sense from a viewpoint of separation, where each person or thing appears to have its own exclusive identity.

You are overlooking an interim step between yourself and your Self. You will not jump directly from where you now believe you are to awareness of Self without first entering a state of complete peace of mind. It is from there you will receive a glimpse of the remembrance of your Self in reality. Many in your world have chosen a path of reverence and deep meditation in order to achieve this state of peace, and a number have succeeded, because it was their clear will to do so.

It need not take lifetimes for this achievement, but it does require a singleness of purpose. However you cannot achieve this alone. You have never *been* alone. We have told you this. From your current mindset your single purpose is forgiveness. Forgiveness of everything. Your Guide will join you in this purpose and be the means by which it is accomplished. Your dream will be forgiven away. It will not be condemned and *then* forgiven. From this place of forgiveness you will be shown a forgiven world. It will appear to be the world you saw in dreams, but nothing in the world you now see will have ever sinned. Then you will recognize a vision of reality you never saw before. The world will be truly beautiful and alive to you, as if never seen, but newly born.

We understand your desire to know what you will awaken to. You want a comparison so you might decide if you really want to leave the dream, or settle back into it, since that seems to be a choice for what is known. You still want to choose from *within* the dream. Yet you want a clear picture of what is outside of it before you choose. Perhaps you can understand that if you had a clear vision of what is outside your dream, you would already be awake and would have already chosen.

How many Sons of God are there? Our answer is not likely to be clearly understood from within a dream of separation. Yet you have asked and we will answer. There is One Son of God expressed in infinite ways. You are a Son of God. What God creates is a complete extension of God with nothing lacking. God is Whole and creates by extending Itself. How can we describe the Self of you who are everything, and *share* everything, to one who prefers a dream of littleness and isolation?

96

Voice For God

How does Oneness interact with Itself?

We admire your tenacity. It is important for you to understand that we are not trying to keep things from you. We have stated this before. Yet you ask as if you can receive an answer, and understand it completely, from within your dream. Whatever words we might use to answer your question would be essentially bereft of the depth of feeling and scope of comprehension required to give them any real meaning to you at all.

Yet once again you have asked, and we will see what we can do. You are wondering what relationships are like in Heaven, and how there can *be* relationships in Oneness. It seems to you that one separate thing must relate to another separate thing in order to have a relationship. If they are the same thing, they are just the same thing, and that is that.

By not knowing who you are and believing you are one tiny personality in a body, you cannot fathom the concept of *being* everything. Even in your imaginings you tend to concentrate on the physical. Your idea of everything might include the universe and all the bodies, planets, and other "things" within it. Yet we have told you all things are projections of minds that choose to experience the very worlds and circumstances they project. You chose the dream you made, to include what relationships should look like within the idea of separation. Your amnesia lets you believe this is reality.

Now let us try a new form of amnesia. Erase all thoughts and concepts of form and physicality from your mind entirely. We are now in abstract mind. There are no bodies and no things. But there is *complete* awareness. Immediately you want to know of *what* you are aware and begin to conjure up the physical. The idea of your mind *not* engaged in specifics is just too abstract. Yet if you can arrive here, you can begin to grasp a glimpse of what, "I Am the Alpha and the Omega," means. You are at the Alpha. At least, let us say you are. You are at the point of potential creation before projection.

Mind creates, and only Mind. The physical does not create more of the physical. Dreams do not create themselves. And you did not create yourself. Relationships in dreams have dreams as their foundations. Bodies cannot join and become as one. Minds can, and do, because their Source is One Mind. It is within this One Mind that all real relationships take place. They have been called holy relationships because they are holy, being of the Whole. Abstract minds are aware of their wholeness at all times, because they are aware they are excluded from no other mind, and none is excluded from their own. It is this lack of exclusion that *makes* them whole. And here, and only here, can honest relationships take place, because God is within them, and they are within God.

And they are love. And they are loving. No thought of non-acceptance or exclusion enters. Thus the concept of fear does not exist. Joy you cannot comprehend abounds when everything communes with everything, radiating to all minds, which in their joy, become as One in Mind.

Voice For God

What is my question?

You want to better understand Oneness, and we do not begrudge you this. Though full understanding of Oneness remains impossible from within a dream of separation, the remembrance of Oneness is our ultimate goal, and your willingness and desire to attain this is all we have asked.

We can at this point only communicate to you in terminology that you are able to comprehend. So we speak to you of minds, as extensions of the One Mind. To you, this implies that separation has already occurred. Therefore you believe, and *want* to believe, that God must have created the separation Himself, by this extension. You still cannot grasp the idea of Wholeness extending Itself as more Wholeness. You believe that each extension must have an identity of its own, or at least a signature of sorts, in order for relationships to occur. It is as if you are asking, "Are you the same Wholeness I talked to yesterday?"

There is no yesterday in eternity. All time is no time. Yet what you are really asking for is familiarity of *recognition.* This you believe is required for relationship. And it is. The Whole recognizes The Whole.

Let us take a step back and relate this to your world in your dream. You believe you are a person, relating to other people, or nature, or things. In reality, you are an idea, relating to other ideas, which appear to be separate from you. Bodies, and all forms of physicality, appear to be proof that all is separate. Yet we have said that all awareness is experienced in mind, and nowhere else. What does it take for minds to join? How can ideas be kept from sharing themselves with all other ideas except by *belief* in separation, by means of special, individual, *exclusive* physicality?

Your world is unnatural and requires tremendous effort to maintain. Oneness flows like waters of the ocean, breathing with the tides and always seeking its own level and merging with itself. This is abstract mind.

It is difficult for you to see another person as yourself because you do not want to. That is not why you came "here" into your dream. Now you are gradually beginning to open to the possibility that all minds are connected, and all ideas are shared. Yet you still require a concept of whom you are sharing ideas with. And who is the you that is sharing? You feel you must envision an identifiable you and an identifiable "other," even if both are whole. You want to know how to recognize the Son of God, or whole Self, beneath, or behind, the physical image of the person present. This has been called the face of Christ within each.

For you, the idea of Great Rays has been particularly helpful. The concept of rays implies some manner of vibratory frequency, whether it is of matter or non-matter, or the shifting between both. You realize there are infinite possibilities of frequency combinations, but any particular combination would be identifiable within the whole. This, to you, could represent the "light body" of a Son of God. Perhaps the signature, or signal, of his calling and receiving is analogous roughly to the carrier tone of any particular radio station. Thus identifiable relationships could take place between, and among, the Sons of God. And these joyous meetings would be broadcast to all of creation. All would be able to tune in at the same "time," and in each such moment of eternity, be joined as One.

This has been meaningful to you and has been beneficial to you on your path to awakening from your dream. It is not necessary for us to disturb this aspect of your belief system. We will only add that what actually *is* Everything, is already tuned in to everything, *as* Everything.

Voice For God

What is heart?

Here is a word with many meanings for you. Is it really your desire to have us define it, and simplify and condense it into one meaning at the expense of all others? Perhaps you would ask us to define spirit, for you closely associate the two.

You have envisioned the heart of you as the "place" where feelings and emotions are experienced, and you have often perceived the two as the same. Let us look at feelings and emotions. You have read that emotions are feelings with judgment attached. This is not an inaccurate statement. Feelings are indications that life is within you and that you are alive. If life is within you, then God is within you, because these two *are* the same.

Emotions are what you *do* to your feelings when you decide what they *mean* according to the belief system you have established for yourself within your dream. Perhaps you would care to ponder where accuracy of perception could possibly be found within this scenario. Since you *give* meaning to everything you experience, you *establish* your own emotions accordingly.

What if you did not have to do this? What if it is not your job to decide what *anything* means? Can you see you would be set free of *giving* a function to everyone and everything you see? You have been playing "make believe" relative to yourself. What you *want* to believe about everyone and everything you have *made* real to you. And your emotions are always produced accordingly. Now we can perhaps realize that how you "feel" about someone is based simply, and *only*, upon how you have judged them relative to you, in your world. This you can change and it is this that you are changing.

Yet if you leave all judgment behind, it appears you will leave all emotion behind as well. Would you not be like a robot? You have long been concerned that you have perhaps *been* a robot for some greater power. A pawn with a devil on one shoulder and an angel on the other, like the old cartoons. You are pushed and prodded and put into impossible situations, then watched to see if you are good or bad and make the right or wrong decision. But *can* you make the right decision in an impossible situation? Or for that matter, a wrong one? The real question is how you can *be* in an impossible situation. It *cannot* happen in reality. It can only *seem* to happen in a dream.

What happens when judgments and their associated emotions are gone? Feelings are still there. But they are totally free of condemnation and fear. When condemnation and fear are not present, what is the only feeling that can be experienced? Only love, in all its infinite manifestations. Here you are in your heart, and here is your heart in you. The spark of life within itself, aware of its aliveness as all.

Voice For God

Am I an avatar for my higher Self?

You have control issues. And we mean that literally.

You indeed appear to have given control of yourself away. You have given it to a character in a dream you forgot you are dreaming. You can take it back. And we are here to help you, when you make that decision *without reservation.* You can take back control because you never lost it. You still have it.

You would still like to be a victim of someone else's decision. It seems inconceivable that you would have put yourself in the place where you seem to be. It was not your *intention* to put yourself in the place where you seem to be. Yet it is the inevitable *result.* You cannot pretend to isolate yourself from everything without eventually feeling isolated. In time. And it is within time where you appear to be isolated.

Let us try something. We will ask a question or two. How can you feel isolated in an apparent world of billions of people, countless animals and plants, and many natural wonders? What are you missing? We will give you time to contemplate.

We are back. Could it be that you do not feel truly connected to *any* of it? Your choice for a separate you led you to experience an entire world of separation, with everything apparently being excluded from knowing the true reality of anything "else." It could be no other way. You have received as you have asked. And as a reminder, we will ask you one more question. Where does this all take place? We will let you give this response to yourself.

You want to know if you are an avatar of your higher Self. What if you were, *now*? What would you do, even in your dream? What if you represent your Self now, in your dream, and have all the power of that Self? This Self, in turn, has all the power of God, because God creates only by extending Itself. We ask you now that, if this is true, and it is, what will you do? Take as much time as you would like on this one.

Perhaps you do not know what you would do. Maybe you would save the world, but you do not know exactly how to do it, or even what that means. With all this power, how could you be sure you do absolutely no harm to anyone or anything? How could you make your dream the happy dream we told you awaits your unequivocal change of mind?

Perhaps you need a Guide. Perhaps this Guide could represent your Self until such "time" when you recognize that you *are* your Self.

Voice For God

What does it mean to save the world?

Deep within, you actually *do* know this answer. Yet you want it verified. And we will do so, with some added flavor. You also feel the means for its accomplishment is beyond your current availability to attain. We will show you that it is not.

You save the world by perceiving a new one, and thereby escape the world you perceived before. And your world literally changes before your eyes. Where you saw hatred, you will see love. Where you saw death, you will see life. Where you saw enemies, you will see only friends with whom you would join. Yet you need someone to see this with you, or your seeing will not be real. We will see it with you until such time when all your seeing is shared.

You save the world by seeing it forgiven. You do not yet understand how to do this because you made your world to be guilty, that you might be innocent within it. This is the character you chose to play in your personal story.

Thus you cannot see your world forgiven, and still hold on to your world. You must relinquish your world in exchange for a forgiven one. To do this, you must become the child who realizes he knows not what he does and knows not what anything means, or is for. You must come with only the willingness to be shown what you do not know, and the simple desire for peace. It is then that you will allow us to help you on the path to reach the goal you actually want.

We will show you that everything in your world is there to be forgiven. And the means will be provided you, at the mere cost of your desire for peace. We will see a forgiven world *for* you, if you will join us in that seeing. For you will join us in purpose. And that purpose cannot be denied, because God established it.

And now the added flavor. The world is already saved, awaiting only your awareness that this is so. How can this be? The memory of God is within you as the Holy Spirit. He is also in every living thing that believes it is separate from God. He thus *experiences* every thought of separation *and* every loving thought within every being who thinks he walks alone. And He is the means to discern between the two, preserving the love, and releasing the rest as meaningless.

He is beyond the limits of time, as is your reality and the reality of every living thing. He sees every dream from its end, as well as every step along the way. He is the conduit through which all of life becomes a portal to all of life. Thus even *dreams* are connected through Him, so the reality of them can be maintained and given meaning through His coordination. The only reality in dreams is the love expressed and received within them. And this He preserves, because love is eternal. The Mind of God deemed it so.

When you join the Holy Spirit in the purpose of joining, all He knows becomes available for your journey home. And what He knows excludes *nothing,* for all dreams are already ended in eternity, as is time itself. Hold this purpose and your path will be made easy, for it has already been walked. You will not walk alone, for all figures in your dream will leave it with you. And the joys of *this* journey will be shared by all.

You have called upon us as the Voice for God. In doing so, you have called upon the Holy Spirit, and are being answered in a manner you can understand. Would you see what remains of your dream when your world is saved? Step back from leading the way. You know not what you do.

You will find that it is you who have been the added flavor all along. For the saving of your world will be experienced in your mind. Then open yourself to receiving the feast of all flavors, within the Mind of God.

Voice For God

What is the meaning of my dream last night?

Before sleep you have had the practice of surrendering your thoughts to Guidance. Last night you asked the Voice for God for guidance as to Whom you should surrender your thoughts. You heard, "Why don't you try surrendering to your Self?" You did so. Let us review your dream as you recalled it upon awakening.

You found yourself standing aside a busy intersection not far from a corner. You felt a desire to cross to the other side, but heavy traffic with turning vehicles kept blocking your progress. You then noticed someone in the center of the road, between the flows of traffic, attempting to come to your side of the road, perhaps toward you. You had a somewhat delayed realization that this one was an aspect of yourself. Still wanting to reach the other side, you found that somehow you had actually done so and were standing out of the roadway surrounded by low growing ivy. You became vaguely aware of two or three somewhat familiar people near you in the ivy, but felt the need to move on to meet someone else at the corner. Now you realized that the place you had left from on the other side of the road was also covered with ivy, or low vines, as was everything that was not roadway. You again felt the need to move to the corner to meet someone. You then realized the one you would be attempting to meet was the one who had made his way to the center of the road in an effort to perhaps reach you on the side you had just left. Again you became aware that this one was an aspect of yourself. You then awakened.

You knew that this dream was significant and began to interpret it. Then you stopped and asked for guidance.

Years ago, you believed you made contact with your Self. Affairs seemed to go relatively smoothly for a period and you found a reasonable peace of mind. You even felt you experienced a few moments that bordered on the miraculous. You asked questions of your guidance, at times believing you received appropriate answers, and at times not. But you never truly joined with anyone or any aspect of your life to the extent of *becoming as one.* Thus you had never truly found your Self.

Your dream was a graphic display of where you have been looking. All images in dreams are symbols, as are all images in your world. The same is true for every word ever written or spoken. They are merely representations of the meanings that lie beneath them.

What would you have the symbols of your dream represent? For you will decide the meanings they have for you. You seem to be looking for your Self outside of yourself. Yet outside of yourself is where all dreams are projected to be. Perhaps the ivy represents the tangled vines of thoughts that constantly inhibit your progress and seem to follow wherever you go. The traffic might represent the ever-present danger on your journey.

What about the people in the ivy you overlooked while on the mission to meet the Self that always seems to elude you? Perhaps you have been overlooking both a way out of the dream and a way of finding your Self at the same time. You now know that all characters in a dream represent you, because you manufactured them. It is *your* dream. Why not join with them and simply awaken as one? As your Self?

Here is your issue. Your nighttime dreams are symbolic mirrors of the waking dream world you made. And this dream you did not make to join with anyone, but just the opposite. In this world, all would be separate from all and you would be the symbol for the central character in perhaps a heroic epoch. Now the drama seems to fluctuate between comedy and tragedy, with you having no control as to the outcome.

Given this purpose of separation, do you see why you *must* overlook others who appear to be wandering through the ivy like yourself, even if they seem to be somewhat familiar? If you truly recognized them and joined with them, you would know them as yourself, and thus as your *Self*. Then what would happen to your dream of separation? Yet you have forgotten that the purpose of all your dreams *was* one of separation.

What if you had a new purpose? You do not have to manufacture it. It *is* your purpose in reality to be joined with everything *as* everything. You need not create the means to awaken to this fact. Guidance awaits only your willingness to be guided and your willingness to relinquish your *self* as guide. The guide that led you to your dream world will only lead you to more dreams. It is the dog that chases its own tail. As always, what you want will direct you to what you perceive. For with your desire, you will have chosen your guidance as well. Seek only peace and you will be guided to the end of all dreams. The Self you seek waits at the center of the road that leads away from *all* dreams. He will come to you when this becomes your goal.

Voice For God

Is all guidance personal?

All guidance is personal to those who believe they are persons. We must reach you where you believe yourself to be, as we have said. What you are questioning is the form, or nature, in which guidance has the ability to make itself known. You wonder about delegation of guidance to angels or other entities, as well as the manner in which guidance is delivered.

You address us as Voice for God, but perceive us not as a voice but as a thought that enters your mind in response to your thought of inquiry. Sometimes the thought from us is quite clear and flows freely. Other times you must ask and wait. You now realize you are not waiting for us, but for yourself to become free enough of preconceived concepts so as to be able to receive information perhaps not currently within your belief system.

There are no limits to how we communicate, except the ones you impose. We are not hiding from you and have no formal structured procedure that must be followed in order for you to reach us. Any sincere communication from the heart, without an attached framework of acceptable responses, will be answered. Your expectations on how the answer should be received will unfortunately, from your perspective, have a great influence on whether or not you believe you are receiving an answer at all.

114

As you are quite creative in ways to appear to hide from reality, we are creative as well. There is nowhere we cannot reach you if you call. We know where your mind is, for there is nothing outside of the Mind of God. This is true regardless of what an aspect of mind may temporarily believe and have attached itself to. What seems to sleep must awaken, because there is no death. So sleep must end in life. Thus angels of death have no function outside of dreams and all demons vanish when the dreamer awakens.

When the dreamer calls to Guidance for angels of life, they may be directed in any form or manner that is helpful and that will not frighten the dreamer. The manner in which dreamers awaken is as unlimited as the dreams they appear to dream. You may put your faith into a certain pathway to awakening, yet we can assure you that, ultimately, *all* pathways lead to awakening. Yet why delay by insisting that your pathway be as you perceive it should be?

Again, all that is required is your willingness to be free of the dream you made. You do not need to establish the acceptable nature of your release. Nor can you. This only makes the dreamer an obstacle to release from his own dream. Step back and *let* your dream be released and you will be a witness to your own awakening. For you will witness the movement of yourself from the personal to the all inclusive and all sharing.

Voice For God

What is an honest witness?

An honest witness does not see with the body's eyes, which were made to see separation. An honest witness does not think with the mind that chose the idea of separation. An honest witness is the child who does not know what anything is for, but merely asks in innocent perception, as a world of grace and beauty unfolds before its presence.

Would you be an honest witness? Do you believe you can be one and still maintain your preconceived concepts, judgments, and conclusions about what everything means relative to who you believe you are? For this is the witness you are to the world you now see. The closest you come to being an honest witness now is if you meet a total stranger and somehow manage not to make judgments about how the person looks. Even if this is accomplished, as soon as the person speaks your personal data bank will begin to identify and separate characteristics into more familiar categories in compliance with your past life experiences. You begin to give the person an identity that is meaningful to you. Or you may simply dismiss the encounter as irrelevant to your life. Your goal is almost always to see the other person as not *like* yourself.

Are you willing to envision everyone you encounter as being without a past? For the past you think each one may have is simply one you have manufactured within your own mind. It can *have* no other reality. Which means the past you gave them has no reality at all.

Yet what if everyone you encountered was someone you knew you wanted to join with simply because you knew that, at some level, you *were* joined with them? Would you be so quick to judge if you knew you were judging a part of your own identity? There would be no thought to keep part of yourself away from yourself. You would be free to express love to another aspect of All That Is. And this is the reality each body would keep hidden.

We will witness this reality beyond bodies together with you, if you are willing to see with our vision instead of your own. It is the vision of unity of purpose, where only love is extended and received. It is where what is now unbelievable becomes actuality. It is the expression of truth and it is the miracle of joining. It is where you are born again into the unity of your Self. For this joining extends to all of creation, which is joined again when any two are joined in the Name of God.

And this you will witness.

Voice For God

Have I experienced miracles?

You ask this because you want to know what a miracle actually is, how it is inspired, and by what means it occurs. You wish to be able to differentiate a miracle from what is simply an unusual and highly improbable occurrence.

You have heard the statement "there are no accidents," and wonder if everything is scripted, including miracles. If so, it would appear to raise the age-old question of free will. Is it free will to choose between illusions as you dream? We remind you that you *gave up* your true free will when you imprisoned yourself by identifying yourself as a character in a story *you* scripted. So now what you really want to know is whether or not you scripted miracles as well. You want to know if the prodigal son not only planned the steps on his path away from home, albeit forgetting he had done so immediately upon embarkation, but also planned the steps of his own return in the process.

What if this is what you did? Would you want us to confirm that for you? People asked as to whether or not they would like to know the time of their own death have generally said they would not. Would you like to know exactly when your dream ends, and how, and *then* continue to play your part? If we somehow ended your dream for you before you were ready, would we represent guidance or the controller of your dream?

Let us, perhaps, ease your mind somewhat. Within eternity, how many plays and scripts and characters could possibly have been produced, and within how many timelines? Do you believe it is impossible for timelines to intersect and overlap? Perhaps you are beginning to get a hint of the size and scope of the playground you have chosen. What are the limits within dreams, except that they must eventually end in awakening?

What we can tell you is that when you appear to advance within your dream, all others you are aware of will advance with you. Miracles allow you to jump between timelines. The prodigal son can choose a path that leads more directly to home, or remain doggedly on his own path. Miracles are already simply there, awaiting your call to not remain where you are. You call for them, and we are the means to ensure your call is answered.

Now you may say that you have called, but have not been answered. But what have you called *for*? Was it for yourself alone in your dream world that you called for a miracle? Would we confirm your idea of separateness? If your dream is to be changed, then all figures in it must be changed as well, because they are all a part of you. Miracles are for all and are shared, or they do not fulfill their function of joining that which appears to be separate.

You experience miracles every day. Each time you share a kind thought or a smile, your timeline shifts slightly and you are on a new path with a new script. It is so seamless you do not notice. But you do notice that you feel better. You have no idea how much you have progressed, for you have advanced in coordination with everyone in your world. And everyone in your world is everyone in your dream.

Do you have any idea what your life, as you know it, *could* have been like had you not experienced miracles throughout? You have been protected at every step. When an aspect of your mind attached itself to the thought of separation, the result *had* to be the projection of fear, isolation, and eventually death. This, the separate ego seems to represent. Yet death is real only within time. And time itself is not real within eternity. And *you* are eternal. Your reality cannot *be* an ego regardless of what you pretend to be in dreams.

The miracle of Life assures eternity for all life. *There is no death.* What seems like death is simply the end of one dream and the beginning of another. As long as the mind remains attached to the belief in the possibility of separation, and the *desire* to experience what it may offer, you will dream lifetime after lifetime. You are playing in the dark. But now you are becoming weary of frightening yourself with what is unreal.

As you call for, and receive, help in awakening, you will come to realize you have never *not* been offered miracles. The shortest path away from your dream has always been placed before you. Yet your ability to recognize it has been totally obscured by your desire to remain the separate self you believe you have created.

You cannot go backward now for you have chosen to awaken. When you do, you will recognize that all the obstacles that seemed to hinder you in your goal of attaining specialness in isolation were always available there to be changed to save you from it. Then you will understand the meaning of gratitude. For you will comprehend the nature of the Savior to Whom you are grateful. The path to your awakening has never been blocked by anyone but yourself. You are always offered the opportunity to witness the miracle of a forgiven world.

Voice For God

What is completion in God?
Is everything already over?

Your question is in regard to timelines as we have addressed them. You wonder whether every timeline has already been completed and, if so, why begin them again.

Everything is complete within God, because nothing is outside of God. Yet we have told you that time itself has no meaning in eternity.

Here it is essential that we review again the nature of truth and illusion. Truth is love expressed. Love expressed is shared by all of creation. It is not limited by boundaries of any kind, to include timelines designed specifically to carve a bit of eternity out of the whole, and then pretend it *is* the whole. In truth, love is the only thing that can, and does, extend beyond the boundaries of timelines, simply because love cannot *be* contained. It is all that remains when your story has ended in time. It is an aspect of your reality returned to your Self, and experienced in Light. Thus it is experienced in all of creation.

Illusions can be expressed as anything that appears to be less than whole. That would be anything that would appear to not be aware of itself as part of, and joined with, everything. We use the word "appear" because, in truth, everything *is* aware it is part of, and joined with, everything. It cannot

122

not be what God created it to be. Yet you were not denied the freedom to *pretend* you could be aware of yourself as less than everything. That is the dream, the story, and the timeline. And all dreams begin and end within the beginninglessness and endlessness of eternity.

So you see, we can envision all dreams having ended, all dreams just beginning, and all dreams in progress, in this moment of the eternal now. In your case we can say that, yes, your dream has ended. This is true outside of time, where your whole Self awaits only your recognition that attempting to have a special piece of nothing that is real, cannot favorably compare with the joy of sharing everything that is.

Your dream *has* essentially ended, because you have chosen to awaken. You have made the commitment. Your progress will be impeded only by your attempts to find your way out by yourself. Yet you still have a concern. You wonder if you might awaken only to begin another dream, and then have to go through this process all over again. We can tell you that, in your awakening, you will come to a clear recognition of what dreams are and what reality is, and you will easily be able to discern which is which.

Let us ask you a question. Do you believe you *own* the part you play in your story? Could no one "else" play the character you are playing within the play? Perhaps only one actor in all eternity could properly play the part of Hamlet. Then he could "own" the part. It is not our goal to attack your specialness. You have placed a call to awaken, and we are responding to that call. Perhaps, though, you can see why we suggest that you may wish to lighten up.

What is complete in God *includes* what appear to be illusions. We have told you there is nothing outside of God and that includes everything that might pretend to be outside of God. In this sense, illusions might be considered pieces of the whole that do not appear to be aware that even they are part of the whole. Also in this sense, all stories that have been told before will be told again eternally.

Voice For God

Can you further clarify the relationship of the
Father with the Son?

First, understand what you are attempting to
do. You are attempting to comprehend the reality of
God, and your Self, from the perspective of a
viewpoint that appears to be outside of God. You
want to comprehend Everything from a place
outside of everything. You can see this
comprehension will be lacking by definition. Yet
your willingness to awaken is all we have asked of
you. So let us respond as simply and clearly as
possible, realizing full depth of meaning still awaits.
We will begin where there is no beginning and end
where there is no end.

Thoughts are infinite in nature, with no
function except their own extension. All thoughts
have always been and will always be. Thoughts are
simply possibilities awaiting activation in mind.
Ideas are thoughts that have been accepted, and
thus activated in mind. They therefore become
available for expression. Expression occurs when
one aspect of mind *shares* the idea with another
aspect of mind. This sharing *brings* the idea into
existence as an experience witnessed by aspects of
mind joined in purpose. By doing so they now
become as one.

Spirit may be considered the idea of
unconditional, all-inclusive love. This idea awaits

acceptance and activation in mind before it can be expressed. Again, one aspect of mind must share the idea with another aspect of mind to bring it into existence as an experience to be witnessed by both. When aspects of mind share *this* singleness of purpose, they bring into existence the experience of sharing unconditional love with each other. And since this love is all-inclusive, this sharing includes all of creation. The feelings and magnitude of this experience we will not attempt to describe. The idea of unconditional, all-inclusive love has been brought to life.

Mind chooses which thoughts to accept and activate into ideas for expression. It supplies creative energy to put the idea into motion and, ultimately, into existence and experience, when united within itself in singleness of purpose.

The Mind of God has always been. It was possible and so It is. Your search for beginnings and endings will only appear to be fruitful in dreams. God may be considered the Idea of unconditional, all-inclusive Love made manifest in Mind. And *nothing else.* Nothing else, because what is all-inclusive includes all.

The Idea of God lives by extending Itself as unconditional, all-inclusive Love. This extension has been established, in your understanding, as the Son of God, or Christ. We have stated that this Son is expressed in infinite ways, each containing the Wholeness of the abstract Mind of God, as well as being contained within It. These Sons, or minds in service of spirit, have also been represented as the Thoughts of God, or as the Great Rays. The fact that each represents the Wholeness of God, as the extension of God, guarantees their absolute equality, one to the other. There can *be* no competition in reality, since each mind is given all in its creation as an extension of All That Is.

This Sonship, in its completion, represents the Father, or unconditional Love made manifest, as the Living God *experiencing* Itself as It extends Itself. This is your purpose as a Son of God. This is why your mind was created by God to serve spirit, the idea of unconditional, all-inclusive love, *and nothing else*. This is co-creation with God.

A fragment of your mind chose something else. Since there *is* nothing else, it chose to make something else by manufacturing a special self in a separate world. Something less than everything. It chose to explore the idea of separation. It chose to explore impossibility. What but chaos could ensue? The idea of separation, when expressed in form, would *appear* as an incomprehensible cosmic explosion. Believing the explosion happened first, and *then* asking the mind to explain the reason why, represents the first, and fundamental, reversal of cause and effect. Welcome to your world.

Now enter the Holy Spirit, or if you prefer, the Spirit of God. What is the Spirit of God? It remains the Idea of unconditional, all-inclusive Love. The Mind of God *maintains* Its eternal creation, extension, and expression by way of Its experience *as* the Living God, through the Eternal Son. Yet if an aspect of the mind of a Son of God seems to choose the impossible, it would appear that their connection has been broken. It appears that Father and Son are no longer in direct communication and communion. Perhaps Heaven has been shattered and has lost a war to the idea of separation.

The Holy Spirit *is* the connection to every aspect of mind which chooses to dream of separation. It was created by God as the Answer to every impossible dream of specialness and death. God creates only Life as an extension of Its Own Life. What God creates is eternal, as is Itself. And God created you. You are eternal. He placed the Holy Spirit within the heart of your mind, as your spirit. Thus He gave you your Identity as unconditional, all-inclusive love. The Holy Spirit will help you remember this, because He remains literally within your being. Thus, must *all* dreams end, ultimately, in awakening and not in death.

So what becomes of the prodigal son when he returns home? The idea that the Sonship is eternal does not mean that the Son can never become a father. God extends His Fatherhood to the Sonship so that creation may be eternally extended. As the Son becomes as One with the Father, he shares the Will to create *like* the Father. Love must be extended to remain all-inclusive. Life must live and expand to know Itself as being alive. There is no end to this in eternity, as there is no beginning. Yet within eternity all is complete.

And when the Father and the Son are in direct communication and communion, what is to become of the Holy Spirit? Is He no longer needed as a connecting link? Perhaps the creations of the Sonship, in Fatherhood, will include a prodigal son.

Voice For God

Can you further clarify the Holy Spirit's function?

The Holy Spirit is God's assurance that no mind He creates can be lost to death through the idea of total separation. It is His guarantee that Innocence cannot be lost through children's dreams of unpardonable sins. The Holy Spirit is the *pattern* for the return of every prodigal son from every journey, in every dream.

The Holy Spirit is the eternal cord that cannot be broken. It is the assurance that nothing can be outside the Mind of God. Yet it maintains the *purity* of the Mind of God in service to unconditional, all-inclusive Love. It represents the Spirit of God as the spirit in you. It knows God's Mind, Which created It, and It is aware of the fragment of yours, which thinks it created itself. Thus It represents the Mind of God in you, as well as spirit, until you return to the awareness of your Self.

The Holy Spirit is the eternal light in you that can never be extinguished, having been placed there by Holiness Itself at your creation. In this sense, it is the life of you within a dream of death. It holds your memory of God and awaits your call to be taught what memory is.

When you call, the Holy Spirit will answer in the manner that you are most likely to comprehend within the role you are playing in your timeline.

There are *no* restrictions on how this may occur, but you often place restrictions on what, and how, you are willing to hear. Sometimes It is a voice in your mind. Believing you are a body, the answer may appear to come through other bodies. For He will change the body's purpose from one of separation to one of joining. Be assured *all* are teachers. The message may appear through a timely song, on a page of a book, or through any meaningful "coincidence." Answers to your call, like miracles, occur regularly and naturally, not awaiting the presence of your ego awareness. Yet the effects are experienced throughout creation.

What most inhibits your awareness of the Holy Spirit's response to your call is your belief that the answer is only for *your* benefit. The Holy Spirit will only answer a request to join, not a request for further separation. Your mind indeed cannot serve two masters. Your request to awaken to your Oneness, and *still* remain a separate exclusive self, can only end in the confusion you now often experience. When your desire to awaken to everything includes *sharing* everything, including your Self, then the answer you receive will demonstrate that everyone must win and no one can lose. The Holy Spirit sees every timeline from the end, so it is only the Holy Spirit Who can make this happen in time.

The Holy Spirit can provide a clear path of awakening from *any* point within *any* timeline. He offers you a new script. He offers a script based upon resurrection in oneness, rather than crucifixion in separation. If it appears to you there are infinite scripts of crucifixion, know there are as many scripts of resurrection. You may always choose again to look at how much you value your story and the separate self you appear to have made within it.

The Holy Spirit is God's Word made manifest in you and is the only reality *of* you within your story. He is the source of love expressed within you, because *His* Source is God Himself. He will lead you to your Savior within your dream. He is the only reality of *any* character in *any* dream. When you recognize Him in anyone who now appears separate, you will have saved yourself. For the idea of separation will, itself, be exposed as the impossibility it has always been and will always be.

You will be saved and you will be free to save. For you must set free all in your dream whom you have imprisoned within your mind. The Holy Spirit is within each one, and He will join Himself within each, and therefore accomplish for you what you know not how to do. All this because it is your will, now aligned with the Will of God. Thus it cannot be denied.

Voice For God

What is the Grace of God?

The Grace of God is the Life of God expressed within you, and as you. It is the completion of every dream through forgiveness, and thus your total release. It can be aided by no effort on your part except your willingness that it be so. It is your will joined with the Will of God. It is the Idea of unconditional, all-inclusive Love made manifest in Mind. And it is your birthright given to you in your creation.

When you receive the Grace of God, you are given the right to extend It. It can only be extended in Wholeness and unconditionally, without exception. It is Life extended, knowing Itself as all life. It is the eternal light in you which cannot be extinguished. It is what you awaken *as* because it is what you have always been.

Yet in your awakening, you will experience a renewed luster and light. You will be born again in Christ. And Christ will be born again in you. The idea of unconditional, all-inclusive love will be extended *as* you. And you will know that it is with infinite expressions of this idea that you are joined. This is the Christ expressed and is Itself the Living God, as One with the Father. Life merges with Life and there is nothing else.

This is the meeting place of the Alpha and the Omega. This is Christ's completion, which makes

God complete. And it is from here that Life and Love are extended eternally, without end. God created you as the eternal when He established your mind as an extension of His unconditional, all-inclusive Love. Thus you travel forward and backward, through every timeline, and experience all resurrection from every dream of crucifixion. And you know your Self in Heaven *as* the Kingdom of God. And all is shared among the infinite extensions of God. For each has been released through the infinite Grace of God.

The Grace of God is why no cause of fear is ever real. There is *no* loss. There is no loss in reality, and there is no loss in dreams, for there is *nothing* outside the inclusiveness of the Grace of God. Dreams are nothing more than bits of reality stripped from reality and presented as the Wholeness of reality Itself. Even no *dreams* are lost. They simply merge back into Wholeness. It is only within Wholeness where meaning lies, for it is here where everything is in unconditional loving relationship with everything.

Do you see why the fear you feel for the loss of your dream cannot be real? All you can lose is your belief that your dream is the Wholeness of all reality. You lose the belief that your story is the only story that really matters. You lose the belief that only you can play a special part in a play, among infinite eternal plays. And you lose not one trace of love expressed, and experienced, within your dream.

The full awakening to the realization of this comes through the Grace of God. These words will be as nothing to the fullness of your awakening. For the Grace of God is complete. It includes the awakening of all dreamers from all dreams. And this all will *experience* as the risen Christ.

Voice For God

What does it mean to renounce the ego?

You are aware that the man, Jesus, renounced the ego and aligned his will with the Will of God. It must be made clear that he did not *denounce* the ego, thus condemning it and giving it a reality in separation. For he had come to realize it did not exist in reality.

You are asked to do the same, if you would escape your dream of a separate specialness and join all of creation in the sharing of all of creation. Why would you not choose this? You *have* chosen this. You have chosen to hear the Voice for God within the Holy Spirit, and once this choice is made, it will not be reversed. For the call has been received by the Answer that must answer. *You* have even renounced the ego. This is the reason you have been able to *receive* these words.

Yet you wonder why the ego still seems to be present. You wonder why you still seem to choose the idea of separation, which remains appealing to you. You move in and out of relative states of clarity and joining, only to fall back into patterns you find immensely difficult to release. Your beliefs and patterns have been so ingrained, you feel the complexity of your current situation would require such an exhaustive search for specific causes that the process of dismantlement could appear beyond your ability.

The process of release *is* beyond your ability. It is time for you to accept this. You believe you *have* accepted this, but you seem to keep forgetting. You are not forgetting. You have not *totally* accepted the fact that there is no hope in finding salvation by imploring remnants of an ego that was designed specifically to *maintain* the dream of separation.

The perceived complexity of your situation is merely an excuse to remain within it. To you, it represents the known. Though at times painful, it is not yet extensively unbearable. Must it become so? What is the real cause of your reluctance to accept release from illusions now as your single purpose and to rely upon the guidance being offered?

There are not many causes but only one. It is the fear you associate with the finding of God. Your venture will have been in vain if it has no purpose. And all you valued will be meaningless. Your journey may now seem a foolish impossible dream, but it was not without purpose. The Holy Spirit has found a purpose within it and would now share it with you. Your purpose is to help release all who dream as you have dreamed. You do not know how to do this because you have yet to escape your own. But the Holy Spirit *does* know how. And working *through* you, He will show you that helping others escape from their dreams *is* the escape from your own. *For you have been holding them within your dream.* Let the Holy Spirit show you how to release them, that you may be free.

You need not wonder how this may be accomplished. This is what the Grace of God is *for*. The joy you will experience with this singleness of purpose, shared with the Holy Spirit, you will perceive as your own resurrection. This is the justice of God. And all who are released will be one with you in Christ, as Christ is One in God. Thus is Love and Life extended eternally. And God is.

Voice For God

What is Forgiveness?

Forgiveness is your resurrection. It is your doorway to release from every dream of separation and death. From within your dream, it is something that you do not know how to do, because you still believe your dream is real. And what *is* real cannot be forgiven, but only recognized as reality.

Forgiveness is your recognition that your dream is not reality. You will resist true forgiveness as long as you still want your dream to be real. Thus you now forgive by first condemning what you believe actually happened, and then searching within your heart for the means to find the goodness to rise above the event that occurred. You will overlook entirely the fact that the event occurred only within a dream of separation, which itself is not real. This form of forgiveness has meaning only in dreams of condemnation.

The part of your mind that made your dream, and would maintain it, is now giving way to the reality of you that is awakening to the fact that there must be a better way, and there must be a way to find it. You are now becoming aware that to escape your dream, you must begin from within it, but be guided by One Who knows it is already over.

The Holy Spirit, with His vision, sees your dream from its end. And all those who appear to share your dream, while lost in their own, does His vision encompass as well. He is the Answer to all dreams, no matter the form they appear to take. He is the idea of unconditional, all-inclusive love that remains within the heart of you eternally. His function is to forgive your world *for* you, when you align your will with the Will of your Creator.

Give your mind to this purpose, and only this, and your world will be transformed before you. Let the Holy Spirit lead, and follow as an astounded witness to your own resurrection within a wholly forgiven world. What do you think you would see now, without projections of your own guilt and judgment attached?

Give your world to Him Who represents the only reality within it. And watch everything you thought was there become innocent of your judgment upon it. Then what was feared and kept apart will be experienced in a light you never saw before. A forgiven world is one of joy, and you would join with all you behold. For everything within it would know of only forgiveness and joining.

This is the happy dream to replace your nightmare. And everyone within your dream will appear to have moved with you to this happy place. For it is the Holy Spirit within them Who will have responded to your call for completion, as well as their calls to you. The call of love to love must always be answered, and can only seem to be delayed by dreams within time.

You are not responsible for the manner in which total forgiveness provides salvation for everyone within your dream. You are only responsible for your willingness that it be so. What is already done, cannot be difficult to do.

Your newfound world will reflect reality. And it will be as Heaven on earth. There will be nothing to fear, for no one will be excluded. No thoughts will be hidden, for all thoughts will be of love and sharing. Minds will relate with minds and bodies will be replaced by light. This forgiven world will host the Living God. It will linger for a while, as the word forgiveness itself begins to lose all meaning.

Voice For God

Is Christ God?

In our efforts to help you understand, we have presented God to you as the Idea of unconditional, all-inclusive Love made manifest in Mind, and nothing else. To the extent that your idea of Christ would fulfill these requirements, then Christ is God. To the extent that your reality fulfills these requirements, then you are God.

Yet can you see that God would be you, and God would be Christ, and All are the same? Where is the hierarchy when the Creator extends *Itself*? All are the same. When unconditional, all-inclusive Love is expressed, it is the Living God. The Christ is the *Expression* of the Idea of God in infinite representations, known to you as the Sons of God, Thoughts of God, or the Great Rays.

More to the point, your questions are, "When does the Son become the Father, or co-creator with God? Does Christ merge with the Father?" We are saying that when the Idea of unconditional, all-inclusive Love made manifest in Mind is *pure,* It *is* the Father, and *must* create by extending Itself. Its purity is a condition of Fatherhood.

Yet when the Mind of God extends Himself in minds, He grants them freedom of will. Otherwise they might consider themselves prisoners within the Mind of God. Thus within the idea of everything connected by, and as, love to everything, there is freedom to explore the idea that there may be something else. That something else could only be the idea of that which is less than everything, expressed as thoughts of separation.

This is why only the Christ Who is complete retains the purity to create like the Father in It's Own Fatherhood. In It's purity, It *is* the Father. So what is impurity within the Sonship? It is simply any aspect of mind that God created which would entertain the idea that a thought of separation is real, attainable, and desirable. It *is* attainable only in dreams. Yet when the Son desires it, he is not denied and held by force within the Mind of God, which is Freedom Itself. The Son is allowed his misadventure in his own personal story. And his amnesia makes it seem real.

But dreams of separation always end in the ultimate separation of death. And this the Giver of Life eternal could not allow. He created the Holy Spirit, the remembrance of the Idea of God, Himself, to accompany the wayward traveler. God, Himself, could not go with and maintain His purity. But He assures that the minds He created cannot lose remembrance of their Source simply by denial within their dreams. The Holy Spirit quietly accompanies, and waits to be called upon with eternal patience.

And the call must come in time. For it is only an aspect of the Son's mind which is asleep and dreaming it is alone. The Self remains with Christ in

His completion outside of time, assured the Holy Spirit will perform His function when called upon.

It is within this release through the Grace of God that the Son is reborn in Christ, and Christ is reborn in the Son. And as all of Heaven rejoices in this celebration of Oneness, who will raise the question of who is Father and who is Son? And what shall we single out to call God?

Voice For God

Are these words meant to be shared?

Everything is meant to be shared, because everything *is* shared. Yours appears to be a personal journey, yet all dreams are the same in content when they share a purpose, even a purpose of separation.

The ones you see as separate are in *your* dream, and how you seem to experience their presence depends entirely on the meanings you give them within *your* mind. Yet each "other" you see represents the entire idea of separation itself, as long as you would keep the gap between you. Mind fragments dream of fragmentation and this is the only thing they would share. For this is the only thing that would keep them from joining.

You have the power to change this. The Holy Spirit is within you, as He is within each aspect of mind which would believe it is not whole. Walk away from your ego and let yourself be led by the Holy Spirit Who will recognize Himself within the one who seems to be separate from you. Thus the one who appears separate becomes your Savior from your dream. In your recognition of his wholeness, you will recognize your own. What has joined through the witnessing of spirit made manifest, will have no need for words. Your will to join will be reflected in ones who appear not to realize they have chosen separation. The Holy Spirit will reveal how the completion of each is included within the other.

The concerns you have for the sharing of these words rest upon former beliefs that still linger. You feel that you do not yet live your life according to this guidance which you receive. You will thus be exposed as not practicing that which is given here. You fear that if you do not represent the application of the information you received, the validity of the messages themselves will be laid open to attack, as well as your worthiness to receive them if they are true.

Leave us only with your willingness for now, for if you lived in complete accord with this guidance, you would no longer *be* in your dream. It is not up to you to defend the words of guidance you have received. All you could defend would be your questions. Should you be asked if this guidance is all in your mind, you may feel free to answer with a simple, "Yes." You need not defend us. For defense is attack, and we attack no one.

Nor is it up to you to decide whether or not you are worthy to receive salvation. God establishes the worthiness of every living thing in its creation. And salvation of all is experienced through His Grace.

Those who are meant to seek and find these words will benefit by them. Those who are not, are on another path, the outcome of which is as certain as your own. None are left behind.

Your willingness to listen is all we have asked. And we give thanks to you for opening to the guidance of your Self.

Voice For God

What is it that is still not adding up in my mind?

You cannot comprehend how everything can *be* everything through interconnectedness. You want to experience this in your conscious mind, which *excludes* the abstract, because it was made separate by you for the purpose of specifics. This was your goal in your "private" dream to establish a special and personal kingdom of your own.

Let us attempt to make something more clear to you. The Whole is greater than the sum of Its parts. *It is not going to add up.* Not from your perspective of a limited specific consciousness. You are attempting to take the whole of everything and squeeze it down into a neat package that will make sense to a tiny fragment of mind. This mind still wants to exclude itself from being, and *sharing,* everything. It does not add up because you still want to do the impossible. The mind in which you are attempting to make things add up is not your whole mind. It is not your Self.

Let us address the real issue of what is not adding up, from your perspective. You still want to know why you have chosen your dream. And specialness alone is not a good enough answer for you. You feel that if the Living God must extend Itself as unconditional, all-inclusive Love in Mind, then creating minds in which to extend Itself makes sense. Yet *how* minds can be created and be eternal themselves, to the inclusion of all timelines, you cannot yet comprehend. Perhaps you can recall your not too distant "past" when you could not have conceived of the massive amounts of information that can be stored within a small computer, with access to a cloud of additional, seemingly limitless, data. And how easily this can be downloaded to another instrument that shares a purpose and speaks the same language.

Maybe you can accept this parallel to the idea of the extension of creation, but you realize that someone had to collect the data in the first place and make it available. Then it had to be formatted for interpretation and meaningful use. You believe that data collectors within creation could be represented by all the prodigal sons bumping along in their seemingly separate lives. Then God, or the Holy Spirit, could somehow extract what is meaningful. By now you realize that all that is meaningful is love expressed. Perhaps these loving experiences could represent facets of the life of the Living God. Or at least a Son of God, if enough of these experiences were put together in a congruous flow. Thus you might have many lives, and the essence, or love expressed within each, can somehow be fused into one "perfect" life of a Son of God. You have used the analogy of pieces of a puzzle that lack full meaning on their own, but when properly connected, produce a beautiful whole picture.

Continuing forward within this vein of thought leads to certain implications. The prodigal son and his journey now have a *purpose.* This may not replace the idea that a fragment of mind wanted to be special, but it may provide an additional reason for the journey that is both beneficial and noble. To you, it may even explain creation itself. Would not the Living God of unconditional, all-inclusive Love require something to extend Itself *to*? What better than to a mind that appears to be less than loving and far less than all-inclusive? This could represent the process of the Living God eternally staying *alive.* The idea of unconditional, all-inclusive love would be reborn, and given renewed life, upon the return of each prodigal son to the father. Thus the idea of separation itself would seem to have a purpose, and actually be required for the extension of love. All this not withstanding our previous very basic attempts to address Oneness relating to Oneness.

Now let us disclose the reason why you want so much for your belief system, as we have just presented it, to be true. If it is, then you have a reason to feel less guilty than you now do. The depths of your guilt you do not realize. You truly believe you are guilty within the eyes of God, and your own. When we revealed that it was your own desire for specialness within a special world that made possible the appearance of every difficulty you now seem to encounter, you took it less as an explanation and more as an accusation. You must have sinned against the Will of God. But if your journey and all such journeys are *mandatory,* you are absolved of all guilt, no matter your desire for specialness.

There is a counterpart to this scenario. If you are not guilty, then God is. God must *cause* His Son to suffer these painful journeys. Yet we are reminded in the parable of the prodigal son that one son remained home with the father. There must have been the presence of choice. So we are back to questioning why you chose this journey, if specialness is not the only reason.

The word compassion comes to mind. You indeed *are* learning to have more compassion for all those who appear to be journeying with you, attached to an idea of separation. You wonder if perhaps God did not *give* you enough compassion in your creation. Surely you can see it was not *needed* in your creation *as* everything. What would you have compassion for that was not a part of you, and you of it? Yet compassion has value while dreaming. You learn not to condemn. And that which is not condemned is set free. In your mind it becomes available for release, through forgiveness, by the Grace of God.

What you release releases you, when you learn how to set free. You become reacquainted with the nature of your Self through the Holy Spirit within you. You will begin to *look* for innocence rather than guilt. And it will be innocence that you recognize, and nothing else. You will know truth and you will easily discern illusions, which would attempt to represent truth. And you will condemn nothing, but merely recognize everything as it is. You will be a witness to all creation, and you will hold all creation together by the love you witness to.

You will realize that perceiving innocence in one cannot make another guilty. God is Innocence Itself, by nature of what God is, and must always be. You are innocent by the Nature of God. When you perceive by this nature, you will behold the innocence of all of creation. For you will be looking from within it.

Perhaps you can see that we have come full circle from the first question you asked which opened our communication, "Am I Forgiven?"

All are forgiven or none are forgiven. If you are guilty, so must God be. If God is guilty, there is no hope for you. When the Idea of unconditional all-inclusive Love made manifest in Mind excludes *nothing*, what can It be made guilty of?

Even within your dream there are those who now recognize your divinity. But you will only become aware of it when you are able to recognize theirs. This will be the beginning of the happy dream for you. For you will no longer be playing alone in the dark. And you will realize that your pathway to escape your dream was always available there before you, no matter which way you turned.

And you will begin to see from the vision you attain in this happy place that there is no alternative to the fact that, ultimately, everything always adds up.

Voice For God

Is my journey one of transformation and progression?

You have made it so in your mind and so it is for you. Your question is one of movement. You feel yourself moving from one level of conscious awareness to a greater level and wonder if this will be eternally so. Thus you are concerned you could spend an eternity within the process of awakening and yet never truly awaken.

We can tell you that completion exists, and is your reality, but not within the confines of your linear conscious mind. Progression of the ego within consciousness indeed can seem eternal. This would guarantee the continuance of the dream and establish the ego, itself, as eternal. Yet the ego is nothing more than a thought of separation, which the mind that thinks it has become attached to. The mind can let this thought go. The mind *will* let this thought go, because its Source is the Mind of God, Which *knows* nothing can be separate from Itself or anything It creates.

Your progression and transformation within your journey need not be so slow. It will seem endless as long as you continue to choose separation. What is your purpose *now*? This is all that matters in the moment. When your *only* purpose is to awaken to the remembrance of all connected to all, through, by, and *as* the Love of God, you will witness the transformation and progression of yourself and your world. You will have aligned your will with the Will of God and you will be on a new journey. And all you perceive will be on the journey with you. You will leave nothing behind, except old and tired ego thoughts of separation.

Open your mind to miracles. Allow the key to the door of everything to be turned for you by the Holy Spirit Who is within you. Call to your Self and your Self will answer. It awaits only your awareness that It is your Identity, which has always been and will always be. Then you will find there is no Identity that is separate from you or of which you are not a part.

Enjoy your journey now. You have made enough payments of dues within your dream. To continue to pay would be to continue to make it meaningless. Now it can *have* meaning. For the meaninglessness of crucifixion and death is being replaced by the truth of resurrection and life. You are the witness and the Holy Spirit is the means within you.

Allow the happy dream to come forth. Let the Holy Spirit show you Himself within every living thing you behold, so you may behold its life. And behold your Self within each.

Voice For God

What else would You have me know?

We would have you know what we conveyed to you long ago, in a moment of peace, when you were not yet able to accept the fullness of its meaning.

You are love and you are loved.

And you have no more meaningful function in Heaven or on earth than to extend what you are, and recognize the fullness of that extension.

Voice For God

Could I please see a kinder, softer world?

Yes. Together.

We will be born again together in every instant, free of the past. And we will bring the universe with us where ever we go. You see, you do not have to attempt to better yourself at all. Just let All That Is experience every universe with you, and through you, as the flavor of you. There is no glorious awakening for one that does not belong to all.

Epilogue (From Guidance)

When you finally recognize the radiance of your brother hiding in the darkness, you will understand it was your own light within that was the means to see.

Made in the USA
San Bernardino, CA
19 September 2016